Betty Crocker's

BOOK OF
FLOWERS

How to Arrange, Decorate and Cook
with Fresh Flowers

PRENTICE HALL

NEW YORK · LONDON · TORONTO · SYDNEY · TOKYO

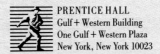
PRENTICE HALL
Gulf + Western Building
One Gulf + Western Plaza
New York, New York 10023

PRENTICE HALL and colophon are registered trademarks of Simon & Schuster Inc.

BETTY CROCKER is a registered trademark of General Mills, Inc.

Library of Congress Cataloging Card Number 89-60706

ISBN 0-13-073610-4

EDITOR: Krystyna Mayer
DESIGN: Bridgewater Design Ltd

Manufactured in the United States of America

10   9   8   7   6   5   4   3   2   1

First Prentice Hall Press Edition

CONTENTS

INTRODUCTION

W hether it takes the form of a lavish bouquet or a child's hastily picked handful, the gift of flowers never fails to delight, celebrating as it does the best things in life and helping us through the worst.

Anyone with even the smallest patch of ground to cultivate can grow a few flowers, and if this is not possible then there are market stalls, flower shops or a flowering pot plant on a windowsill to enjoy. Just a few sweet-pea plants will yield bowlfuls of flowers all season long, and one small rose bush will provide fragrant petals for use in any number of wonderful recipes, pot pourris, lotions and scents, prolonging the smell of summer into the grey winter months.

The life of a flower may be brief, but there are many ways in which this can be extended. The blooms can be dried or preserved, used to add flavour and scent to food, and pressed into service as fragrant decorations for the home.

In the next six chapters dozens of suggestions are given for growing and using flowers. There are projects for special occasions and useful hints for presents, methods for making wedding bouquets and scented writing paper, unusual recipes and cooking tips, in fact all manner of ideas that will often surprise and hopefully always inspire you.

R oses are among the oldest and best-loved flowers in cultivation. They are invaluable in flower-arranging and other decorative schemes, and are widely used in pot pourris.

Chapter One

PICKING
AND
DRYING
FLOWERS

*G*arden flowers are most often grown simply for their beauty or fragrance, but they can also be planted as a crop for picking and preserving. Indeed, in the past, large country houses had part of the kitchen garden set aside specifically for cultivating flowers for indoor use, and though nowadays few people would do this, it does make sense if you grow vegetables to plant a few rows of flowers alongside them. Choose some easy annual varieties that thrive on being picked regularly. If your garden is not suitable for this kind of cultivation, do at least reserve a corner or two for plants that will provide flowers for a particular purpose, such as cutting, drying or eating. A plant of lavender or rosemary is a must in every garden, and there should always be room for a climbing honeysuckle, a good fragrant rose, and perhaps a hydrangea. A tub of marigolds or nasturtiums will add spice and colour to a summerful of salads, and a tripod covered with sweet peas can be squeezed in among perennials or shrubs to provide scented blooms for cutting all season long.

Of course, if you have no garden at all, you can buy all manner of wonderful flowers from a market stall or flower shop and even save the finished blooms to make your own pot pourri.

A PLACE FOR EVERYTHING

With just a little imagination and skill it is possible to grow a large array of useful flowers in any garden. Where they are positioned counts very much towards their success, so you must be aware of their needs before you plant or sow.

Nearly all the half-hardy and hardy annuals thrive in full sun and an open but sheltered position. Some, such as nasturtiums, enjoy poor conditions, giving far more flowers on starved, thin soil than on a rich, fertile one. Most of the sub-shrubby plants like lavender and rosemary, which have their home in the Mediterranean area, love full sun and well-drained soil. Some flowers may want cool, shady positions, but the majority of those grown for drying, cutting and cooking like plenty of light and air.

Once you have established the conditions a particular plant needs, you can decide where best to put it. It is sometimes easier to manage a group of plants, cornflowers, say, if they are arranged in a straight row, so that any treatment, for example tying or staking, can be carried out quickly and efficiently, as with any productive crop. A special perennial such as the spectacular sea holly or eryngium always looks good in a herbaceous or mixed border, combining or contrasting with other plants, and though you might cut all its flowers for drying it will still make a good contribution to the complete garden.

Try growing culinary flowers such as marigolds in among herbs or the vegetables they may accompany on the table, and always when planning a garden think about leaving small spaces for planting several extra tulips or lilies for picking, so that you do not have to raid a precious part of the ornamental garden. Allow a few flowers – the opium poppy, for example – to go to seed for interesting seed-heads, and leave a few leeks or onions to flower in the vegetable garden. They dry to great, pale-pink globes, and of course an artichoke left to open is superb fresh or dried, if you can bear to forgo the eating of it.

Top: Poppies have beautiful, bowl-shaped blooms, and interesting seed-heads once flowering is over.

Above: The distinctive heads of the globe artichoke dry well and provide a striking addition to a mixed border.

Far left: Cheerful, brightly coloured marigolds are excellent as cut flowers and also last well on drying.

HARVESTING FLOWERS

nowing when to harvest flowers for different purposes is very easy once you have had a few seasons' experience, but here are a few guidelines for those new to growing and gathering.

Fresh flowers to be brought indoors for arrangements and decorations are best picked in the early morning or evening, rather than on a hot, sunny afternoon, when they will naturally have less moisture in their cells through transpiration and therefore be more prone to wilt later. As flowers always benefit from a long drink or conditioning before they are used, this may determine just when they are gathered. Ideally, a drink overnight is perfect if they are to be used the next morning, so evening picking is probably best. Always choose fresh, healthy blooms just coming into full flower, or in a slightly open bud, if you prefer.

Harvesting flowers for drying and preserving can be more tricky. Certain types, such as helichrysums and other crisp immortelles, are basically dry even before they have been picked, but they must be cut well before they are really open as they will continue to unfold after harvesting. After picking, helichrysum buds should immediately be wired (page 102), the wire rusting into position and taking over from the weak stem. Other flowers for drying, such as peonies, larkspur, roses and achillea, are best gathered at midday when the blooms are as dry as possible, obviously not on a wet or very humid day. Cut one type of flower at a time, strip off any surplus leaves and bunch the stems if necessary.

Very sharp, high-quality secateurs are good for any kind of flower harvesting, but for small, soft-stemmed plants such as chives, scissors are usually the best tool for the job.

FAR RIGHT: The tall, strong stems of achillea make a superb display in a herbaceous border and dry well.

Annual asters have a long flowering season, are easy to grow from seed and make perfect cut flowers.

Helichrysum bracteatum comes in a vast range of brilliant, glowing colours and is an essential dried flower.

AIR DRYING FLOWERS 1

*C*ommercially, most flowers are dried quickly in highly controlled conditions, yet often a rose or peony picked from the garden and air dried in a warm kitchen will finish up in a better state and with a much stronger colour than its mass-produced equivalent. Certainly, many flowers can simply be hung to dry in a warm place with no other treatment needed. This means that if you have even a little space in an airing cupboard or over a kitchen range you will be able to preserve all kinds of flowers very satisfactorily. The only things you will need to remember when drying are that the air must circulate around the flowers to speed the process, that it must not contain any moisture (a kettle steaming away on the cooker with flowers hung above it is not a good idea), and that strong light will accelerate fading of the colours. A sunny window is not a good drying position.

Depending on where you plan to do your drying, you can either stretch a string or wire between two points and hook the flowers over this, or make a more elaborate arrangement using rods, cup-hooks screwed into the ceiling, or battens. If you have only a bunch or two at a time to dry, an ordinary wire coat-hanger will make a useful frame.

Large flower spikes such as delphiniums are best left single, but smaller flowers can be dried in loose bunches held together with rubber bands. To hang these securely, make small S-shaped hooks from 6 inch (15 cm) lengths of pliable garden wire. Slip one end under the rubber band and the other over the support.

In the right conditions, flowers will dry in three or four days, but the exact time will obviously depend on the size, denseness and water content of the blooms.

LEFT: Many flowers dry successfully in a warm, airy room. Here, spikes of delphiniums, roses and peonies are hung in a kitchen and dried fast to keep their colour.

Annual larkspur is like a smaller version of the delphinium, but comes in pink, red and white, too. It is simple to grow from seed and can be used fresh or dried.

AIR DRYING FLOWERS 2

*T*he ideal for anyone aspiring to dry their own harvest of flowers would be an outbuilding with plenty of roof space, a very dry atmosphere, good ventilation, little or no light, a felt or metal roof to heat up and warm the flowers underneath, a certain amount of work space for preparing the blooms after cutting, and perhaps even some storage facilities.

If you are lucky enough to have access to some such space, here are a few tips to bear in mind. A large mass of drying flowers will need the moisture emanating from them removed as soon as possible, so some kind of ventilation or window high up in the building must be provided. Lengths of strong twine or wire should be stretched across the roof space and bunches hung from these by wire hooks, while small flower-heads should be slotted through the holes in a piece of fine-mesh wire netting fixed across a corner. This is a particularly good method for flowers that lose their shape when they are hung head downwards, such as those in the daisy family, or blooms like the chives which get crushed in a bunch.

Flowers suitable for air drying include *Achillea mille-folium*, *Alchemilla mollis*, most of the ornamental onion family, *Anaphalis margaritacea*, cornflowers, dahlias, delphiniums, echinops, eryngium, *Gomphrena globosa*, *Gypsophila paniculata*, *Helichrysum bracteatum*, lavender, love-in-a-mist, marigolds, peonies, roses, salvia, statice or sea lavender, and xeranthemum.

Some flowers, for example marigolds, cornflowers and *Alchemilla mollis*, can simply be hung in bunches under cover to dry outdoors. A barn, shed or outbuilding is ideal for this purpose.

DRYING
WITH DESICCANTS

Although some flowers are too delicate or difficult to air dry, they can still be dried in a desiccant. With a little practice many quite unlikely specimens can be treated in this way, but unless you have several boxes of desiccant it will be a slow process, as only a few blooms can be done at a time. Desiccated flowers should keep their shape perfectly, and are particularly useful for decorating pot pourris or for using in flower arrangements, although, if they are to stand upright, they will first need to be attached to an artificial stem (the stalks will usually have been discarded and the heads dried on their own, space being at a premium with this method).

There are many different types of desiccant to choose from, including sand and borax, as well as specially prepared mixtures. Some of these contain coloured indicators that react with moisture to tell you when the powder needs drying. You will also need one or more large, airtight plastic boxes and a few small paintbrushes and tweezers with which to lift and move the flowers around.

Put a layer of desiccant in the box and lay your chosen flower-heads, which should be unblemished and as perfect as possible, on top, leaving space around each. With a brush or spoon handle gently push the powder into and over the petals, working up from the underside of the flowers to make sure that each petal is supported. Completely cover each head and close the lid. Leave the box for a few days in a warm, dry place and check the blooms every now and again. When the flowers are dry but not too brittle, remove them carefully and brush off any surplus powder. They will then be ready for use.

Above: Many flowers can be given the desiccant treatment. These flower-heads, freshly harvested and awaiting the process, include roses, pinks, honeysuckle, scabious and marigolds.

Far left: A selection of perfect flower-heads lies waiting in boxfuls of desiccant powder. More of the powder will be poured over and around each bloom before the lids are closed.

THE GLYCERINE TREATMENT

*F*lowers and leaves that have been preserved in glycerine are not dry – in fact they feel faintly oily to the touch – but they can still be used to make long-lasting decorations and arrangements, whether on their own or alongside fresh or dried flowers.

In this method of preservation, glycerine is drawn up into the plant with water and saturates its cells, preventing any decay. It is a particularly good way of treating the fluffy seed-heads of plants such as clematis. If these are picked at their glossy, bronze-coloured stage and given the glycerine treatment, they will remain in this form instead of exploding into a dull, fluffy mass. Leaves such as magnolia, beech and butcher's broom also respond well to this method, and it is worth experimenting, too, with flowers such as delphiniums and, in the autumn, with stems of berries, preserved rose-hips and blackberries making superb winter decorations.

Cut the stems cleanly and diagonally and immediately place them in the preserving solution (use a tall, thin jar: you will then need only a small amount of mixture for each batch), this consisting of one part of glycerine to two of hot water, mixed together and allowed to cool before use. Leave the stems in the liquid until they have absorbed it. With leaves you will notice a gradual change of colour, beech, for example, turning a lovely mahogany brown, but seed-heads will stay basically true to their original colour.

The soft, silky seed-heads of many clematis varieties are easily preserved with a glycerine and water solution. *Clematis tangutica* has particularly pretty seed-heads, abundant in late summer.

Chapter Two

Preserving Flower Scents

From earliest times people have tried to capture flower fragrances, whether in simple nosegays or for use in other ways. The pot pourri (literally 'rotted pot', from the French) is one good example of how the elusive scents of plants can be preserved. It is a very old method but one that is still thriving: a dish of subtly scented flower petals is as appropriate today in a modern city apartment as it once was in a medieval manor-house.

This chapter explains everything you need to know about the ingredients and techniques used to make the two basic types of pot pourri, and gives several recipes as starting points for your own ideas. Once you begin to make pot pourris and discover how simple it is, you may well find yourself completely absorbed in this ancient and beautiful craft.

THE TWO
POT POURRIS

*O*riginally, pot pourris were always stored in closed ceramic jars, which would be opened only when someone used the room in which they had been placed. The jars would be stood near a heat source such as an open fire, and as they warmed up the lid would be removed to release the fragrance. When the room was done with, the lid would be replaced and the fragrance sealed in once more. Nowadays we tend to want to see the pot pourri and enjoy its wonderful textures and subtle colours, so how it is displayed is an important consideration.

There are two basic methods of making a pot pourri. The moist method is the most authentic, producing a very long-lasting and beautifully scented result, but the pot pourri it makes is not particularly attractive. The second, dry, method is slightly quicker and simpler and the pot pourri extremely pretty to look at, but the scent is not very long lasting, though both types can be revived.

The main ingredient for each of these pot pourris is rose petals, which hold their scent well and are readily available in large amounts. Other flower petals are added for colour and fragrance, along with leaves, herbs and spices, and, when the recipe calls for it, ingredients such as dried citrus peel, seeds, bark and pine cones. One other vital element is a fixative, usually plant based, which fixes the scents in the recipe so that they do not fade, while essential oils are used to reinforce the natural scents and to boost a fragrance if it is faint.

Lᴇғт: All kinds of flowers, whether fragrant or chosen simply for colour and texture, can be used for pot pourris.

Rɪɢʜᴛ: Before drying petals, strip them off their stems, spread them out and sort through, selecting only the best.

MAKING A DRY POT POURRI

*B*ecause commercial pot-pourri recipes often stint on fixatives, which are costly but vital for a good result, many ready-made pot pourris are nothing more than pretty mixtures of flowers and leaves with essential oils added for fragrance. If you have access to flowers that are already scented, such as roses and lavender, and make your own, the result will almost certainly be better and more authentic than any shop-bought mixture.

The petals used to make this type of pot pourri must be completely free from moisture. Either strip the fresh petals from the stems and spread them out to dry, or else dry the stems first and strip them later. The petals can be dried on trays or fine-mesh frames in a warm cupboard, a dry attic room or, faster, in a very low oven. In high summer, when the sun is shining, it is possible sometimes to dry petals outdoors in a very short time, but choose a sheltered spot so that they do not blow away. It is sensible to tackle one type of flower at a time, but if you plan to make only one small batch, then by all means dry all your mixed petals in one go.

Leftover petals and flower-heads from dried arrangements are useful ingredients, and you can even make use of shop-bought blooms once they are no longer needed. Pot-pourri-making does not have to be confined to the summer months, and many spring flowers produce a good base. Try tulip, freesia and daffodil petals, for example. Through the year remember to dry strips of citrus peel and scented leaves such as lemon verbena and sweet woodruff, as well as many of the herbs, such as thyme, hyssop, mint, rosemary, sage and marjoram.

Top: Separately dried and stored, these marigold, rose and chamomile petals await future use in a pot pourri.

Right: Thin strips of orange, lemon or any other citrus peel can be dried and added to pot pourris for their zest.

Cinnamon, nutmeg, coriander, red
peppercorns, cloves and cardamom
can be used whole or finely ground.

Gum benzoin comes in large, hard
lumps that must first be ground down.
Orris root is sold ready powdered.

SPICES AND FIXATIVES

*O*nce you have some perfectly dry flower petals and leaves ready, the next step is to find a fixative for your pot pourri. In the past, many different substances were used for this purpose, but these days most of them are scarce and expensive. In addition, three of the original fixatives, civet, ambergris and musk, were all animal products, whose use today, now that most of us are aware of animal conservation and protection, has no justification, particularly when there is a suitable vegetable equivalent.

The best fixative to use at home, then, is powdered orris root, which is widely available and very effective. It is made from the ground rhizomes of a variety of iris, hence its name. Another fixative quite commonly used is gum benzoin, which comes from the resin of a Styrax tree from the Far East and takes the form of very hard lumps that have to be ground down with a pestle and mortar. Other ingredients that work as fixatives, as well as providing their own inherent fragrance, are tonka beans, oakmoss and vetiver.

Spices are often added to pot pourris as well. Whether whole or ground they allow an even greater variety of scents to be imparted to the mixture. While the main fragrance usually comes from the flowers, spices can provide warmth and zest when used judiciously. A few that are suitable are cloves, cinnamon, nutmeg and mace, allspice, coriander, anise and cardamom. Grind your spices at home, if you can: you will invariably get a better scent than if you were to buy them ready ground. And, if you wish to avoid a slightly dusty-looking pot pourri, use a combination of ground and whole spices rather than powdered spices alone.

*R*ed and yellow chillies, allspice, juniper berries, green peppercorns and cinnamon bark give texture, bulk and colour to any pot pourri, as well as adding spicy scents of their own.

SEASONAL SCENTS

One final thing is needed for a pot pourri and that is essential oil, which both strengthens the natural fragrance of the ingredients and makes available a wider choice of scents. It should be used very sparingly, particularly if it is a good-quality oil: most recipes will need just four or five drops. You will quickly learn how to use it and which scents to choose for the best results.

SPRING POT POURRI

This is lemony and light and a pretty yellow, and makes a delightful mixture for spring.

1 cup chamomile flowers
½ cup marigold petals
½ cup lemon-verbena leaves
1 cup mixed yellow flowers, e.g. tulip, mimosa, daffodil
2 teaspoons ground coriander
2 teaspoons ground cinnamon
4 teaspoons powdered orris root
4 drops vetiver essential oil
A few whole dried yellow chillies, marigold heads or cinnamon sticks, for decoration

The method of making a dry pot pourri like this one is always the same. Measure the petals, flowers and leaves into a large bowl. Add the fixative and ground spices plus any other dry ingredients. Mix them very well with your hands or a wooden spoon. Add the drops of essential oil and mix again. Put the mixture into paper bags, loosely seal and place somewhere cool and dry to cure for 4 to 6 weeks, shaking occasionally. The pot pourri will then be ready for use.

F ar right: This traditional-looking, summery pot pourri includes whole rosebuds, peony heads for decoration, a hint of blue larkspur and a few drops of rose essential oil for an old-fashioned scent.

COTTAGE-GARDEN POT POURRI

1 cup red and pink rose petals and whole buds
1 cup mixed pink and red petals, e.g. larkspur, peony
¾ cup chopped bay or sweet-gale leaves
4 teaspoons powdered orris root
2 teaspoons ground cinnamon
2 drops rose essential oil
2 drops rose-geranium essential oil
A few whole roses or peonies, for decoration

Make this summer pot pourri according to the dry method described on the left.

A bove: A spring pot pourri such as this can have plenty of whole flower-heads for texture, including roses, marigolds, mimosa, helichrysums and tulips, and for interest a small bunch of cinnamon sticks.

MOIST POT POURRIS 1

*M*oist pot pourris have basically the same ingredients as dry ones but are made quite differently. The only extra ingredient you will need is very coarse salt, ideally non-iodised or with no additives.

It takes practically a whole summer to create a moist pot pourri, but the results are worth waiting for. A well-made mixture can last for several years, and even then it can always be freshened and revived by adding a few more drops of essential oil or reviver and re-curing in a dark place for a few weeks. This recipe is for a basic moist pot pourri.

MOIST POT POURRI

10 cups partially dried, highly scented rose petals
3 cups coarse salt
2 tablespoons each ground cinnamon, allspice and nutmeg
1 tablespoon ground cloves
5 tablespoons powdered orris root
4 or 5 drops rose essential oil

Follow the method described overleaf (page 37) to make the mixture.

Above and right: Freshly picked, highly scented rose petals form the basis of any moist pot pourri.

A SUMMER AND A WINTER VARIATION

LAVENDER POT POURRI

Lavender has traditionally been one of the most useful flowers for all kinds of household preparations. It is often used in mixed pot pourris, where it adds its own, very distinctive, clean, astringent smell. Here is a recipe based almost entirely on lavender.

2 cups lavender flowers
½ cup mixed blue and mauve petals, e.g. larkspur, cornflower
2 teaspoons powdered orris root
4 drops lavender essential oil

Use the dry method described on page 30 to make this pot pourri.

WINTER POT POURRI

It is quite fashionable nowadays to change a pot pourri according to the season, so a rich, colourful version for Christmas and the winter months is particularly welcome. Small home-made pomanders made from limes or tangerines add a decorative touch to bowlfuls of this mixture. For a really festive note tie them with lengths of scarlet velvet ribbon.

1 cup deep-red rose petals and whole rosebuds
1 cup maroon-coloured hibiscus flowers
1 cup mixed cinnamon bark, whole cloves, whole nutmegs, mace and allspice berries
½ cup dried red chillies and red peppercorns
2 teaspoons ground cloves
2 teaspoons ground cinnamon
2 teaspoons ground nutmeg
2 teaspoons powdered orris root
½ cup dried orange and lemon peel
2 drops cinnamon essential oil
2 drops orange essential oil

Again, follow the dry method on page 30 to make this version. Finish off with small pine cones and any other suitable pieces of decoration that come to hand.

LEFT: The fresh, astringent scent of lavender makes for a wonderful pot pourri, which needs only a few petals of larkspur or some bright cornflower heads to bring the colour alive.

FAR LEFT: Masses of whole spices and even miniature pomanders have been added to this dry winter pot pourri to give texture, warmth of fragrance and a wealth of rich, glowing colours.

MOIST POT POURRIS 1

*M*oist pot pourris have basically the same ingredients as dry ones but are made quite differently. The only extra ingredient you will need is very coarse salt, ideally non-iodised or with no additives.

It takes practically a whole summer to create a moist pot pourri, but the results are worth waiting for. A well-made mixture can last for several years, and even then it can always be freshened and revived by adding a few more drops of essential oil or reviver and re-curing in a dark place for a few weeks. This recipe is for a basic moist pot pourri.

MOIST POT POURRI

10 cups partially dried, highly scented rose petals
3 cups coarse salt
2 tablespoons each ground cinnamon, allspice and nutmeg
1 tablespoon ground cloves
5 tablespoons powdered orris root
4 or 5 drops rose essential oil

Follow the method described overleaf (page 37) to make the mixture.

*A*BOVE AND RIGHT: Freshly picked, highly scented rose petals form the basis of any moist pot pourri.

MOIST POT POURRIS 2

A moist pot pourri is made as follows, using the list of ingredients given on page 34.

Partially dry some rose petals until leathery. Put a layer of these in a large earthenware bowl or crock and cover with a layer of salt. Continue to layer like this, then place a weighted saucer on top. Every day remove the weight and stir. After about 6 weeks, when the rose petals and salt have turned into a brown, crumbly mass, break them up and add the rest of the ingredients, together with any other dried petals and leaves, as desired. These could include lemon verbena, any of the herbs, lavender, marigolds and jasmine, all of which should be completely dry before being added. Stir well and cure in paper bags for a further 6 weeks, as for a dry pot pourri (page 30). The mixture will then be ready for putting into containers.

Moist pot pourris are beautifully scented but rather dull in appearance, as the colour is not retained in the petals. This means that the best way to display them is either in small, lidded baskets or, if in an open bowl, decorated with plenty of dried flowers, such as roses, lilies or lavender bottles (page 134).

*M*oist pot pourris have a wonderful scent but a rather dull appearance, which can be greatly improved with the aid of a few decorative dried rose heads and leaves. Bright-red blooms have the greatest impact.

SHOWING OFF THE SCENTS

*D*ry pot pourris deserve to be well displayed. Once you start to make your own, you will discover that you can control quite closely the colours and textures in them. This means that you will be able to create a special mixture for a particular setting or colour scheme. The good thing about any recipe, though, is that it will look superb in more or less any situation.

Think of great, Oriental ceramic bowls filled with rich Elizabethan pot pourris on polished oak tables in ancient country manor-houses. The same mixtures poured into a series of shallow, glossy baskets would look stunning arranged on a low table in a simple, modern interior, as would huge pottery bowls in a brightly coloured matt glaze filled simply with lavender, or else plain glass dishes heaped with exotic mixtures of dark-brown bark, seeds, leaves and spices.

The containers in which you choose to display your pot pourris are very important. Baskets always go well with the colours and textures of dried flowers, but you will probably need to line them before filling, as the fine spices and fixatives have a habit of dropping to the bottom of any container. Old china bowls and dishes are always lovely: blue-and-white china looks particularly countrified and pretty with a pinky-red pot pourri, while Eastern ware has just the right richness to combine with the strong colours of darker mixtures.

*R*IGHT: Dried petals, whether scented or not, can be layered in glass containers, colour by colour, for an unusual and lovely effect.

*B*ELOW: This winter display has been created by setting a few miniature cyclamen in a copper pan filled to the brim with a rosy pot pourri.

BOXES AND BASKETS

*I*t is still possible to find interesting and unusual containers for pot pourris. Look out for old tin or wooden boxes in second-hand shops. With a little cleaning up or restoration many can be pressed into new service. Old storage tins designed for spices and other kitchen ingredients look good filled with a suitably spicy pot pourri, such as the one below. This recipe produces a rather masculine mixture, one appropriate for a hall or study, perhaps, or wherever you need a clean but slightly exotic fragrance.

SPICY POT POURRI

1 cup lemon-verbena leaves
1/2 cup rose petals
1 cup whole coriander seeds
1 tablespoon allspice berries
6 whole nutmegs
1 tablespoon whole star anise
1 tablespoon crushed cinnamon bark
1 teaspoon ground nutmeg
1 teaspoon ground coriander
2 tablespoons powdered orris root
4 drops cedarwood essential oil

Use the dry method described on page 30 to make this pot pourri.

Returning to the theme of baskets, another possibility is to decorate the rim of a suitable container with a few flower-heads. Choose fairly solid flowers such as roses, or break up larger heads, for instance hydrangeas, into little florets. Secure the flowers with the aid of a glue gun or blobs of good adhesive or, if you intend re-using the basket in the future, attach the flowers temporarily, with a piece of fine rose wire.

L EFT: This spicy pot-pourri mixture
is displayed in an old canister
possibly once used for storing spices.

B askets make perfect containers for
pot pourris and look even prettier
edged with dried flower-heads.

THE ANTIQUE TOUCH

*A*ntique boxes and tea caddies make perfect containers in which to keep and display pot pourris. Sometimes these wooden boxes are lined with metal, and have a hinged lid that can be left open when you wish to enjoy the scent of the pot pourri, and closed when you do not. All the golden, mellow tones of polished wood look beautiful with dried flowers, particularly when these echo the colours of the wood.

Choose a spicy, earthy pot pourri, or one that has Eastern overtones. The recipe below includes a large number of whole, dried flower-heads for visual appeal, and the scent is warm and spicy, and faintly exotic, too.

SANDALWOOD AND YELLOW-ROSE POT POURRI

1 cup whole yellow rose heads
1 cup whole marigold heads (yellow pot and African)
½ cup mixed bay and lemon-verbena leaves
½ cup mixed yellow petals and flowers, e.g. helichrysum,
dahlia, achillea
3 tablespoons powdered orris root
1 tablespoon dried lemon peel
1 tablespoon each cinnamon, cloves, nutmeg
3 drops sandalwood essential oil

Make this in the usual way (page 30), adding a few other whole flowers or perhaps some small larch cones as a final decoration.

A tiny tea chest makes an ideal
container for any desktop pot pourri.
It can be kept closed for the most part,
keeping the scent in, and opened for
enjoyment when the desk is in use.

Chapter Three

COOKING
WITH
FLOWERS

*I*n the last few years there has been an enormous revival of interest in the art of cooking with flowers. This may seem slightly odd to many people, but in fact flowers have been used as far back as our knowledge of history goes. Indeed, ingredients such as rose water, which is in widespread use today in Middle Eastern countries, were used centuries before the birth of Christ. The emphasis recently on the presentation and visual qualities of food has meant that flowers have come back into the kitchen and are more than likely to stay there. They certainly give the average home cook a chance to be more creative, and to experiment with tastes and textures that suit the modern move towards light, simple flavours and fresh, natural food.

A word of warning before you start: poisonous flowers obviously do exist, so never eat any that have not safely identified as being edible; use only unsprayed flowers.
All the flowers used in the following recipes are fine, but if you wish to experiment, get yourself a reliable reference book first. Remember, too, that many wild flowers are protected or scarce, so resist any old-fashioned recipes you may find for, say, cowslip pancakes, and pick only very common species.

FLOWERS AS FOOD

*A*ny garden, whatever size it may be, will provide enough space to grow even a few flowers for the kitchen. Some of the easy annuals worth planting each summer are nasturtiums, marigolds and borage. Many flowering herbs are useful for both leaves and flowers, so grow a plant or two of hyssop, thyme, marjoram and rosemary. Lavender, surprisingly, is delicious in recipes and a must in every garden, and of course roses are vital for many dishes. Violets make subtle sweets and crystallised decorations, and orange, jasmine and bergamot flowers all produce delicious tisanes and teas. The courgette plant contributes to the savoury range with the now quite classic Italian dish of deep-fried courgette flowers.

In general, flowers should be fresh when used for food, though there are exceptions, such as hibiscus flowers used for teas. Marigold petals dry easily and well, and make a superb addition to cakes and breads in the winter months with their faintly spicy flavour and golden colour. Try warm marigold scones spread with rose-geranium jelly and you will soon be converted to the idea of flowers as food.

LEFT: Nasturtiums are among the easiest annuals to grow, thriving in full sun and poor soil.

TOP RIGHT: Eaten when fresh, nasturtium flowers and leaves make a dazzling addition to many dishes.

BOTTOM RIGHT: Violets, with their evocative woodland scent, have long been used to flavour food and drinks.

A SALAD AND A STARTER

*B*oth these recipes are simple to make and are ideal for a hot summer's day.

HYSSOP, POTATO AND BEAN SALAD

In midsummer there are green beans and cherry tomatoes in the vegetable garden, as well as tiny new potatoes. This pretty and colourful salad goes perfectly with cold meats, but it can equally well be served as a main lunch dish on its own.

(SERVES 6)

3½ cups tiny new potatoes, cooked and cooled
10 ounces fine green beans, cooked and cooled
¼ cup black olives
8 ounces cherry tomatoes
2 tablespoons chopped fresh hyssop flowers and leaves
Sprigs of fresh hyssop flowers, to decorate

Gently mix all the ingredients together and put in an earthenware dish. Over the salad pour a dressing made from 3 tablespoons of olive oil, 1 tablespoon of lemon juice, 1 crushed garlic clove, salt and freshly ground black pepper. Decorate with a few sprigs of fresh hyssop flowers and serve.

T**OP RIGHT**: Herb flowers make pretty decorations for savoury dishes. Here, strips of chive stems have been split in half to make them more flexible and used with the flower-heads as a garnish for a light, refreshing mousse.

F**AR RIGHT**: Many herb flowers are every bit as edible as their leaves. Hyssop has brilliant-blue, sweetly flavoured blooms, used here to dress up a bean and potato salad.

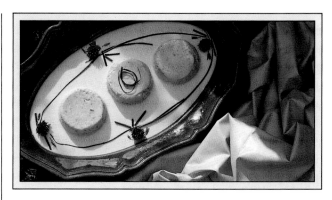

CUCUMBER AND CHIVE MOUSSE

The following is a very light and cooling first course for a hot day. The chive flowers are the perfect edible decoration.

(SERVES 6)

1 large cucumber, peeled
2 envelopes gelatin
2 tablespoons cold water
1 cup cottage cheese
½ cup heavy cream
4 tablespoons finely chopped fresh chives
⅔ cup sour cream
Salt and pepper
Split chives and chive flower-heads, to decorate

Chop the cucumber in a food processor until very fine. Dissolve the gelatin in the water and allow to cool. Add the cottage cheese and heavy cream to the cucumber and process for a few seconds. Add the chives, then pour the gelatin into the mixture and mix well. Finally, fold in the sour cream, season to taste and pour into individual molds. Chill. Turn out on to a large serving dish and surround with a sauce made from ⅔ cup of sour cream thinned with a little milk and 2 tablespoons of lemon juice. Decorate with split chives and a few chive flower-heads.

NASTURTIUM SALAD

Both the flowers and the leaves of the nasturtium plant are hot and peppery to taste. The leaves have often been used as a substitute for watercress and they contain very high amounts of vitamin C. The flowers come in brilliant colours ranging from yellow and orange to deep red, and there are many varieties to choose from: the dwarf and the variegated, or the long and trailing, perfect for hanging baskets. Thriving in poor soil, they make a hot splash of brilliant colour all through the summer, and if left to seed themselves they will re-appear with abandon the following year.

Flower-heads for eating should be fresh, unblemished and unsprayed. Do not wash them if at all possible, as the soft and delicate petals bruise easily. Check in the long horn at the back for lurking insects and pick off the stem. Use the flowers with a variety of summer salad leaves, such as green and bronze lettuce, cos lettuce, and frisée or oak-leaf lettuce for interest.

The salad below can be eaten as part of a meal or as a first course on its own.

(SERVES 6)

SALAD
Mixed salad leaves from several different types of lettuce
About 36 nasturtium heads

DRESSING
2 tablespoons olive oil
1 tablespoon walnut oil
1 teaspoon made French mustard
1 tablespoon white wine vinegar
Salt and freshly ground pepper

Shake all the dressing ingredients together and use as a light sauce for the salad.

Nasturtiums add a peppery taste to a green or mixed-leaf salad, and a flash of contrasting colour.

TWO COLOURFUL STARTERS

The first of these recipes makes a substantial and unusual starter or a light main course. The second is a light and colourful concoction of fruit and flowers.

ZUCCHINI FLOWER PARCELS

Recipes for stuffing the beautiful golden-yellow flowers of the zucchini are common throughout the Mediterranean. This version has the flowers stuffed with rice, herbs and pine nuts and deep fried.

(SERVES 6 AS A FIRST COURSE)

6 zucchini blooms
Olive oil, for frying

BATTER
1 egg
1 cup all-purpose flour
4 tablespoons cold water

FILLING
½ onion, chopped very small
⅓ cup long-grain rice
1¼ cups chicken or vegetable stock
2 cloves garlic, crushed
¼ cup pine nuts
1 tablespoon chopped fresh herbs, e.g. basil, parsley, chervil
Salt and pepper
Flour, for coating

Mix all the batter ingredients together. Fry the onion in a little olive oil, add the rice and cook for 2 minutes more. Add half the stock and the garlic. Cover and simmer, adding more stock as necessary. When the rice is cooked, add the pine nuts and herbs and season to taste. Let the mixture cool. Stuff each flower with a little mixture. Dip in flour, then batter, and deep fry in oil heated to 350°F. Remove the flowers from the oil, drain well and serve.

WATER MELON WITH BORAGE AND SCENTED GERANIUM

(SERVES 1)

1 small water melon
1¼ cups water
⅓ cup superfine sugar
2 strips lemon peel
4 borage leaves
Juice of 1 lemon and 1 lime
Scented geranium and borage flowers, to decorate

Cut the top off the melon. Extract and roughly cube the fruit, then mix with a lemony syrup made from the water, sugar, lemon peel and borage leaves. Simmer, strain and cool. Add the lemon and lime juice, then put the mixture back in the shell. Decorate with the flowers and serve on a bed of vine leaves, if desired.

Top: Southern Europe has many recipes that use the golden flowers of the zucchini plant in their own right.

Right: Sweet geranium flowers and blue borage make a fitting decoration for this deep-red water melon.

FLOWERS FOR TEA

*M*arigolds are one of the basic ingredients in the cake recipe below. In the second recipe, Michaelmas daisies are used as a non-edible decoration.

MARIGOLD CAKE

For this recipe you can use fresh or dried petals. Set out the cake with fragrant cups of smoky China tea served without milk.

(MAKES ONE LARGE, LOAF-SHAPED CAKE)

1 cup softened, sweet butter
1 generous cup superfine sugar
4 eggs, beaten
2 cups all-purpose flour
1 teaspoon baking powder
Grated peel of 1 orange and 1 lemon
3 tablespoons fresh marigold petals or 2 tablespoons dried
Granulated sugar (optional)

Grease and line a 9 × 5 × 3-inch loaf pan. Cream the butter with the sugar and add the beaten egg little by little. Sift the flour with the baking powder and fold into the creamed mixture. Add the peel and marigold petals. Spoon into the pan and bake in an oven preheated to 350°F for about 1 hour, sprinkling with granulated sugar half-way through, if desired. Cool for 5 minutes, then remove from the pan. Serve when just cool. This cake keeps well and can readily be frozen, too.

Left: Marigold petals have imparted a delicate flavour and slight orange hue to this light tea-time cake.

Top right: This glazed apricot tart wears a frothy garland of non-edible Michaelmas daisies, used purely for their decorative effect.

APRICOT TART

This is a classic tart in the French style but decorated with non-edible flowers. If possible, buy triple-distilled orange flower water from a pharmacy or health-food shop.

(MAKES ONE 9-INCH TART)

1½ pounds fresh apricots, halved and stoned
⅓ cup superfine sugar
1¼ cups water
Juice of ½ lemon
2 tablespoons orange flower water
One 9-inch sweet pastry tart crust,
pre-baked for 15 minutes
Michaelmas daisies, to decorate

Poach the apricots in a syrup made from the sugar, water, lemon juice and 1 tablespoon of orange flower water. When barely cooked, drain and put in the tart crust. Bake in an oven preheated to 350°F for a further 25 minutes or until quite cooked and brown. Reduce the syrup by fast boiling until thick. Take off the heat and add the rest of the flower water. Paint over the warm tart, entirely covering the surface. Eat at room temperature soon after cooking. Arrange flowers around the tart as a decoration for serving.

CRYSTALLISING FLOWERS

*T*he method of crystallising flowers described here makes flowers that last for many months, if correctly stored. It produces very pretty and delicious results, perfect for decorating summer desserts and candies or special-occasion cakes. Primroses, violets, roses, freesias, rose geraniums, lavender and honeysuckle are all suitable for this treatment. Larger flowers like roses are normally broken up into petals before crystallisation, while smaller flowers such as primroses and violets are crystallised whole.

METHOD

To make crystallised flowers you will need powdered gum arabic, which you can buy from a pharmacy. It is quite expensive but you need only a small amount. Dissolve a spoonful of gum in a spoonful of rose water and leave until it has become a thick paste. Paint this on to the petals, leaving no gaps. Dip into and sprinkle with superfine sugar and leave in a warm place until quite dry and crisp. A wire-mesh cooling rack is useful for supporting flowers such as primroses while you paint them and also for drying them. When done, store them in an airtight container.

*P*rimroses are among the best flowers to grow for crystallising. Here, they have been used with crystallised violets to cover a very special cake and to top a few tiny fondant sweets.

VIOLET DELIGHTS

*T*he recipe below for a chocolate pudding makes a delicious sweet, not too rich, cooked like a cheese-cake, chilled, then decorated with crystallised violets. Try serving it with a small glass of violet liqueur, or parfait-amour, as it is otherwise known. It is possible to buy this, but you can also make your own. The colour is quite weird and the flavour and scent reminiscent of violet cachou candies, but with a kick.

CHOCOLATE TERRINE WITH VIOLETS

(SERVES 12)

1 cup Ricotta cheese
1 cup cream cheese
1/2 cup superfine sugar
2 eggs, beaten
1/4 cup cocoa
1 teaspoon pure vanilla
Crystallised violets (page 56), to decorate

Beat the cheeses together until well blended, then beat in the sugar. Add the eggs and the cocoa dissolved in a little hot water. Beat in the vanilla and pour into a 9 × 5 × 3-inch loaf pan lined with waxed paper. Set the pan inside a larger roasting pan half filled with water and bake in an oven preheated to 350°F for about 1 hour, or until the top is firm and golden. Remove from the oven and cool. Chill for several hours before serving, decorated with the crystallised violets.

LEFT AND RIGHT: The smoothest chocolate pudding is enhanced by a sprinkling of crisp, crystallised violets and perhaps a dash of the glorious violet liqueur known as parfait-amour.

VIOLET LIQUEUR

(MAKES 2 CUPS)

2 1/4 cups vodka (or eau-de-vie, if you can get it)
50 heads scented violets (Parma are best, or from a florist)
1 cup white sugar
1/4-inch strip vanilla bean

Put all the ingredients in a jar and leave for several weeks, shaking occasionally. Strain through muslin, then through a coffee filter paper, until clear. Add a few drops of purple colouring for an even prettier effect.

FLOWERY FANCIES

T<small>OP</small>: Thick plain yogurt can be garnished with ripe strawberries and a spray or two of flowers and leaves.

R<small>IGHT</small>: These sumptuous home-made truffles have been flavoured with roses and violets and decorated with crystallised petals.

The versatility of flowers is nicely illustrated with these two ideas, the first a luxurious recipe using flowers that have undergone various metamorphoses, the second a way of presenting them at their simplest and most natural.

ROSE AND VIOLET TRUFFLES

To make these delicious truffles, use only the best chocolate, white or semi sweet. Both kinds are prepared from a basic mixture using the same method, but the rose version has a dark, rose-scented truffle centre covered with white chocolate, and the violet version a white, violet-scented centre encased in semi sweet dark chocolate. Put them into tiny petit-four cases and pack a few into a decorative box lined with shredded tissue paper for a superb present.

(TO MAKE ABOUT 15)

6 squares white or semi sweet chocolate
4 tablespoons sweet butter
1 tablespoon brandy plus 1 tablespoon rose water,
or 2 tablespoons violet liqueur (page 59)
6 squares white or semi sweet chocolate, for coating
Crystallised petals (page 56), to decorate

Very gently melt the chocolate with the butter. Add the liqueur and flavouring. Remove from the heat and cool. Roll into small balls and leave to harden. Melt the coating chocolate gently over hot water and dip each truffle in until well coated. Leave on an oiled surface and decorate with crystallised petals before set.

STRAWBERRY FLOWERS

Through the summer months, when delicious plump strawberries are growing, use sprays of fruit and flowers as decorations for summer puddings. Scatter a few across a bowl of whipped cream or thick yogurt to serve alongside a dish of the strawberries on their own.

ROSE-PETAL CREAM

This soft, light pudding is slightly scented and flavoured with roses. It combines perfectly with the tender red fruits of summer – strawberries, redcurrants, cherries and raspberries. Serve it well chilled, either with fresh raw fruits or with a warm compote of mixed fruits poached in a light syrup. Alternatively, mold the cream and turn it out or, if preferred, simply pour it into a glass dish to set. Decorate it with a few fresh, pale-pink rose petals scattered at random over the surface or, for a more graphic effect, use single petals and leaves to lay out a suitable pattern.

(SERVES 6 WITH FRUIT COMPOTE)

1¼ cups whipping cream (or half light cream, half heavy)
1½ tablespoons gelatin
4 tablespoons water
⅓ cup superfine sugar
1¼ cup thick plain yogurt
2 tablespoons triple-distilled rose water
Petals and flowers, to decorate

Whip the cream lightly. Dissolve the gelatin in the water. Beat the sugar with yogurt. If molding the cream, rinse out a 3-cup mold with cold water. Beat the cool gelatin into the yogurt mixture and, working rapidly, add the rose water and cream. Pour into the mold or dish and chill for several hours before decorating and serving.

LEFT AND RIGHT: Soft, creamy puddings look wonderful decorated with fresh rose petals. Whether you use a few petals at random or make a simple design, be restrained and try not to smother the surface.

FLOWER SORBETS

*W*ith this basic recipe for sorbet you can experiment with all sorts of flavors. The result is always spectacular and yet it costs next to nothing to make. Take trouble serving and presenting the finished ice using pretty, glass-stemmed dishes, or put a scoop or two of sorbet on a plate with a spoonful of strained fresh fruit as a sauce. Some kind of crisp or wafery cookie goes perfectly with this ice, and find your smallest teaspoons to savour every mouthful.

BASIC SORBET RECIPE TO FLAVOUR WITH FLOWERS

(SERVES 6)

½ cup superfine sugar
2 cups water
Pared peel and juice of 2 well-scrubbed lemons
Flowers (see below for quantities)

Dissolve the sugar in the water and add the lemon peel. Bring to the boil, stirring, then simmer for 6 minutes. Add the flowers, remove from the heat and allow to cool. Strain, then add the lemon juice, tasting as you go so as not to mask the flower flavour. Freeze in a plastic container for 2 to 3 hours or use an ice-cream-making machine. When the mixture is mushy and half frozen, remove from the freezer and beat. If you do this in a food processor the result will be very fluffy. Freeze again until firm. Allow to soften slightly before serving.

Liqueur can be added to strengthen a flavour, if desired, or poured over the final sorbet. You can also replace the sugar with honey for a different effect. Try it with the lavender flavour and use ¼ cup of honey in place of the sugar in the recipe.

AMOUNTS OF FLOWERS TO ADD TO BASIC SYRUP
Rose petals: 1 generous cup
Lavender: 6 flowering sprigs
Scented geraniums: 4 leaves
Herbs: 12 sprigs approx.

T*OP*: Lavender flower-heads, here steeping in a lemony syrup, may be used to produce an unusual sorbet with a sharp, scented flavour.

R*IGHT*: Scented rose-petal and lavender sorbets make fragrant, delicious desserts for hot summer days and special meals.

SCENTED
GERANIUM JELLY

*S*cented geraniums are wonderfully old-fashioned, cottagey plants that thrive on a sunny windowsill or planted out in the garden in the summer months. Belonging as they do to the pelargonium family, they are cousins of the bright-flowered geraniums seen growing in pots, decorating terraces, steps and gardens almost ubiquitously. The scented types generally have smaller leaves than the common sort, but they are marvellously aromatic. In some, simply crushing a leaf sends out powerful wafts of fragrance. The rose-scented geranium or attar of roses, commonly used in olden times for fingerbowls, is well known, but there are many other varieties, smelling, for example, of lemon, eucalyptus, ginger, balsam, lime and orange.

Lemon- or rose-scented geraniums make the most delicious preserves, served at tea-time with good bread and butter or plain biscuits and muffins. The base is best made from apples.

(MAKES ABOUT 4 POUNDS)

4 pounds cooking apples
3½ cups water
White or preserving sugar
Juice of 2 lemons
15 scented geranium leaves

Chop the apples roughly, leaving the skin, stalk and pips. Put in a large pan with the water and simmer until soft. Strain for several hours through a jelly bag or muslin; do not squeeze the fruit pulp through or the jelly will be cloudy. Measure the juice into a preserving pan and for every 2 cups of juice add 1 pound of sugar. Add the lemon juice and the geranium leaves. Stir over a low heat to dissolve the sugar, then boil rapidly until set, for about 10 minutes. Quickly remove the leaves and pour into clean, warm jars. Cover the jars while the mixture is still hot.

A rose-petal version can be made using a 2 cup measure of petals instead of geranium leaves.

ABOVE: There are many different types of scented geraniums, but the most useful culinary ones are the rose- and lemon-scented varieties. Keep a pot or two on the kitchen windowsill.

FAR LEFT: Capture summer scents and flavours for winter tea-times by making flower preserves. Rich and glowing red in colour, rose-geranium apple jelly is one of the best.

SUMMER CLARET CUP

ABOVE: The blue flowers of annual borage are loved by bees. The leaves give a cool cucumber fragrance to drinks, while the flowers are essential for decorating a Pimm's cocktail.

FAR RIGHT: This cooling claret cup, based on a 19th-century recipe, has a lovely colour that is best seen through a clear glass bowl. Serve it at a garden party or a summer wedding.

Borage was once believed to have a tonic effect and to lift the spirits, but nowadays its most common use is in summer drinks, where the bright-blue, star-shaped flowers provide both a decorative touch and a faint cucumber taste. It is a very easy annual to grow from seed and has a habit of self-sowing itself generously once established. Self-sown plants start to flower in May, often continuing until the late frosts.

This cherry-red wine cup is based on a Victorian recipe. You can obviously make it as strong or as weak as you like, but whatever you do, try to serve it from a clear punch bowl to appreciate the sparkling colour and pretty decoration. Use long tumblers and be sure that each measure contains at least one of the cheerful blue borage flowers.

(SERVES 20)

1 tablespoon superfine sugar
3 cups fresh strawberries
4 small strips cucumber peel
Juice of 3 lemons
3 tablespoons brandy
2 tablespoons Cointreau
2 bottles claret or similar red wine
1 bottle sparkling mineral water, soda or lemonade
Borage flowers and sprigs of mint, to decorate

Dissolve the sugar in a little hot water and place in a large bowl. Slice the strawberries if they are large and add to the bowl with the cucumber strips, lemon juice, brandy and Cointreau. Pour in the 2 bottles of wine and top up with mineral water, soda or lemonade, as desired. When ready to serve, add ice and a liberal sprinkling of borage flowers and mint sprigs.

APPLE-MINT LEMONADE

A century or so ago women often made lemonade in the spring to give to children as a kind of tonic, knowing little about vitamins but believing that it cleansed the system. It was certainly a very good idea after a long winter with little fresh food, and as a child I remember the taste of home-made lemonade as being very special and quite delicious. It is really easy to make, and this version has the refreshing taste of apple mint as a bonus, perfect for a hot, dry day.

Decorate the jug with sprigs of pale mauve apple-mint flowers or, if you prefer, use lemon balm. The lemonade will keep in a refrigerator, but it is best to remove the lemon peel if you intend to store it for long, as the pith soon makes the drink quite bitter.

(MAKES ABOUT 3½ CUPS)

4 lemons
½ cup superfine sugar
2½ cups water approx.
Few sprigs apple mint and/or lemon balm
Mint flowers and sprigs, to decorate

Scrub the lemons thoroughly to remove any wax or residual spray. Peel strips thinly from the skin and put in a heatproof jug. Add the sugar and pour over just enough boiling water to dissolve it. Add the sprigs of mint and leave to cool. Squeeze the juice from the lemons into the syrup. Remove the mint but leave the peel. Top up with cold water according to taste. When ready to serve add ice, if desired, and a decoration of mint flowers and leafy sprigs.

H̲ome-made lemonade is quite delicious as a spring and summer drink, and even better with sprigs of lemon balm and flowering apple mint added for flavour and decoration.

SOOTHING TISANES AND TEAS

As well as adding scent and flavour to conventional teas, flowers can be used in their own right to make tisanes. These flowery infusions have long been taken medicinally as well as for enjoyment, lime being particularly well known both for its delicious taste and its soothing qualities.

Use dried or fresh flowers to make a tisane (1 teaspoon of dried flowers or 3 teaspoons of fresh per cup), steeping them only for about 3 or 4 minutes before drinking. Make all your flower or herb tisanes in a heatproof jug. Strain them into a cup when ready or use a small metal sieve-like infuser to dip them straight into a cup of boiling water.

Other flowers which make excellent drinks are bergamot, verbascum, thyme (both the flowers and the leaves) and marigold. Drink all these plain or add a small amount of honey if you need a sweetener.

Make your own scented and slightly exotic flower teas by adding dried petals to a good China tea such as Keemun or Oolong. Once you have made the mixture, pack it into a small box or pretty tin, label it and use it to make a gift. Otherwise, store it in an airtight container until required.

Buy the best loose tea you can afford and simply mix it by hand with the petals you choose. Try strongly scented red or pink dried rose petals, or dried flowers from the common white jasmine (*Jasminum officinale*). The proportion of petals to tea will depend on how strong you want the flower flavour to be: experiment with 2 tablespoons of scented rose petals to 1 cup of tea, and 1 tablespoon of the stronger-scented jasmine to 1 cup of tea.

RIGHT: Richly scented rose-petal tea is simplicity itself to make, once you have the necessary ingredients.

BELOW: Lime flower tea, really a tisane made from the whole flower-heads, is a most soothing drink.

ELDERFLOWER DRINK

*T*he elder bush has always been a very useful plant for the countrydweller. A country drink worth reviving is elderflower 'champagne', a sparkling, refreshing drink that can be enjoyed on any lazy summer's day. **Use only the flowers in recipes. The stems and leaves of the elderberry plant are toxic. Do not use in recipes.**

Lᴇғᴛ: This sparkling summer drink scented with elderflowers is made from the simplest ingredients.

Bᴇʟᴏw: Elderflower 'champagne' made in the early part of summer can be enjoyed after a week or so.

(Mᴀᴋᴇs ᴀʙᴏᴜᴛ 4½ ǫᴜᴀʀᴛs)

6 elderflower heads, washed and free from insects
1½ pounds white sugar
3 lemons, well scrubbed
2 tablespoons white wine vinegar
4 quarts water
Elderflower sprigs, to decorate

Dissolve the sugar in a little of the water heated to boiling. Thinly pare the lemons and add the peel to the sugar. Put the flower-heads in a large earthenware or glass bowl and add the sugar and peel mixture, the wine vinegar and the remaining water. Stir well, cover and leave for about 4 days in a cool place. Strain off the liquid and bottle. In 5 days or so it should be sparkling. Serve it well chilled in long glasses.

FROZEN FLOWERS

*Fl*owers or petals encapsulated in cubes of ice look wonderfully pretty floating in summer drinks or used as table decorations. Float them in bowls of wine cup or glasses of Pimm's, or pile them around a glass serving dish filled with a cool, creamy pudding. If they are to be used in drinks, then all the flowers and leaves must of course be edible. Try rose petals, tiny sprigs of mint or thyme in flower, scented geranium blooms, primroses, violets, borage and lavender.

To make floral ice cubes, put a tiny flower in each section of an ice tray. Half fill each section with water and freeze solid. Top up with water and freeze again. Doing the freezing in two stages means that the flower will end up in the middle of the ice, its natural tendency being to float to the top of the water. Look out for unusual shapes to make, such as hearts or flowers.

FLOWER ICE BOWL

Another interesting idea is to make a flower-studded ice bowl for use as a serving dish with ice creams, sorbets or soft fruits. Although this is a bit fiddly to make, it looks quite spectacular when finished.

Use two large plastic bowls that will not crack when frozen, one being a little smaller than the other (the difference in size between these will determine the thickness of the finished ice bowl). Pour a little water into the larger bowl, add some petals or flowers, then freeze. Put the smaller bowl inside and tape the rims together to stop it moving about. Fill the gap between the bowls with water and more flowers, then freeze again. If you have time, build the sides up in stages so that the flowers do not all float to the top. Unmould by dipping the bowls quickly in hot water. The finished ice bowl can be stored in the freezer until needed.

Edible flowers and leaves encased in ice make enchanting and unusual decorations for festive summer drinks.

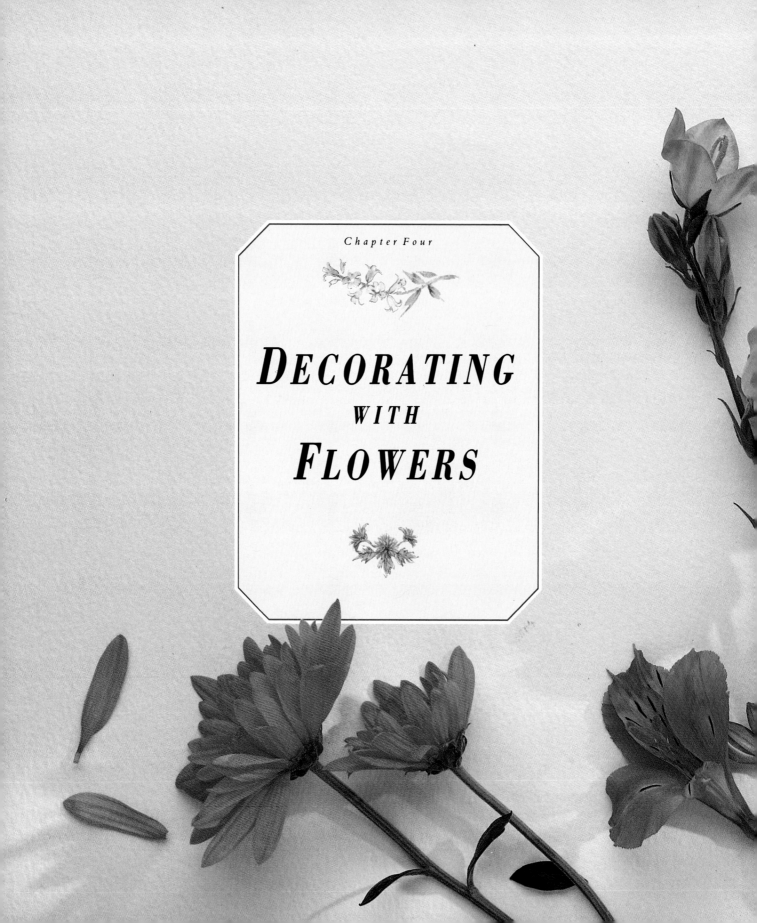

Chapter Four

DECORATING
WITH
FLOWERS

Flowers have the ability to give pleasure at many different levels. More often than not they do not need to be forced into contrived arrangements or lavish decorations, as they will speak for themselves even in the simplest jug or bowl.

Unfortunately, many people are put off by what they see as the mystique of flower-arranging. All too often someone who has great skill and creativity when it comes to cooking, for example, finds that faced with a bunch of flowers he or she does not know where to begin. Truth to tell there are no rules, no mysterious craft that can be learnt only at great length. If you love looking at flowers and enjoy their colours and scents, you are already half-way there.

Forget those great, hotel-foyer set pieces put together like a painting by numbers. Instead, simply use what you have and try to look at everything with a fresh eye. Learn how colour works from seeing how plants and flowers combine in a garden or in the countryside, and collect pictures of flowers or anything that might suggest a way of putting a bunch together, whether it be an old painting or a photograph in a magazine. Above all, enjoy yourself, and learn that a house without at least one pot or vase of flowers is not quite the place it could be, even if the most you can do is provide a jam-jar of daffodils on the kitchen table. And there is not much wrong with that.

PUTTING IT TOGETHER

The only tools and equipment you will need when working with flowers are a good pair of sharp secateurs or florists' scissors, possibly a basket in which to collect material from the garden if you grow your own plants and, if you are using dried flowers, a pair of wire cutters and some stub wire. For conditioning flowers in water before starting on the actual arrangement, a deep, narrow bucket is useful, but an ordinary household one will do, as will a sink or basin.

Fresh flowers are best given a long drink after picking (page 12); most prefer the water used to be tepid, not freezing cold. Cut the flower stems at an angle and split or hammer the woody stems of shrubs and trees to allow the water to be taken up. A few flowers need special treatment for perfect results. All the poppy family should have the ends of their stems dipped for a few seconds in boiling water or seared over a flame. This will make them last a lot longer than they would normally do. Ranunculi benefit from this process, too.

The containers you choose for your flowers are very important to the success of the final arrangement. Build up a collection of plain glass and ceramic ones for simple bunches, and always keep in mind that jugs of any shape, colour and size are among the most useful containers you can have: look out for old ones in secondhand shops, and never scorn a piece of china with a chip missing or some other blemish. It will look fine filled with flowers.

LEFT: With dried arrangements, fillers such as sea lavender and *Alchemilla mollis* are invaluable for saving on flowers in shorter supply and for covering any florists' foam that might show through.

FAR LEFT: Bucketfuls of achillea stand waiting to be bunched and hung, ready for drying.

A HERBAL BOUQUET

*T*here comes a point in midsummer when most of the shrubby herbs have spikes of flowers on them, often in tones of pale mauve, white and blue, with the odd touch of yellow from feverfew, tansy and rue. Rich as they are in nectar, herb flowers are invariably attractive to bees, and when picked make fragrant bouquets that last a long time in water. Many of these flowers, while subtle and unassuming, are nevertheless quite exquisite, and have a charm all their own when used in relaxed and countrified bunches. They are not the kinds of blooms that take to sophisticated arranging or smart containers, but look their best in cosy jugs and plain glass shapes.

Herbs put into clear containers should always have the lower leaves and twigs removed from the stems, since any foliage left in the water will tend to rot and make it go cloudy, thus marring the general effect.

A vase of herbs in the kitchen is useful as well as pretty, since you can easily pick the odd leaf or two while cooking to flavour a soup or perk up a salad. Annual herbs worth bringing indoors for their leaves and flowers are dill, caraway, borage and marigolds, while perennial herbs with attractive flowers include such familiar plants as chives, chicory, winter savory, hyssop, rosemary, thyme, lemon balm, mint, lavender, marjoram, tansy and rue.

Early summer is when many herb plants come into flower. The blooms have a simplicity and subtlety of colour not often exploited in flower arrangements but nevertheless particularly fresh and charming.

FRAGRANCE FIRST

*I*t sometimes seems rather unfair in the plant world that some of the most beautiful flowers also have the most wonderful scents. A lily would be magnificent without any scent at all, but combined with a powerful fragrance its effect is completely stunning.

Some perfumes carry well on the air, and a small vase of flowers such as winter sweet or freesias will fill a whole room with fragrance. Warm, humid air brings out the best from scents, and they are obviously more noticeable in a confined space. A sheltered garden with walls and high hedges, for example, will hold flower scents particularly well, though in many gardens there are times when the air is laden with fragrance anyway, in the early evening, say, or after a shower of rain.

Most flowers for sale in flower shops sadly have little or no perfume, but there are still wonderful things to be found, such as tiny bunches of damp, scented violets in the spring, or lily-of-the-valley and stems of hyacinths. Blossoms such as lilac, which should smell divine, are usually forced by growers for an early market, and this for some reason reduces any scent they might otherwise have. You can usually rely on good old freesias, though, on lilies and on some of the pinks. There seems to be a move, too, towards breeding scent back into florists' roses, which for so many years have smelt virtually of nothing at all.

To be sure of a fragrant supply of flowers right through the year, however, you really have to grow your own. You can sow old-fashioned varieties of sweet peas, which have a truly wonderful scent, and ancient and interesting varieties such as the sweet briar rose, whose foliage, after rain, carries the refreshing perfume of sharp green apples.

LEFT: This tiny posy of miniature pink blooms includes geranium flowers, convolvulus and pretty foliage. The sweet briar leaves beside it have a scent of apples.

Lilies, larkspur and sweet peas make a heady mixture in a summer bouquet. Seemingly exotic flowers such as these lilies are perfectly at home in plain and simple containers.

A SENSE OF STYLE

Choosing how to arrange a bunch of flowers is surprisingly difficult for a large number of people, but it really need not be.

Most often the best approach will in fact be suggested by the flowers themselves. There is no point, for example, in trying to make a sophisticated arrangement out of a bunch of shaggy garden asters or cornflowers. These kinds of plants need simple, cottagey treatments if they are to look their best. Graceful white tulips, on the other hand, grouped thickly in a white vase, have the very essence of style and sophistication.

Scale is also an important consideration. A few of the last roses of summer with their small, heavy heads and short stems, for instance, should be left on their own in something that does not detract from their very frail beauty. Use a few small tumblers from a set and group the roses wherever you will see them close up, on a shelf at eye level, perhaps, or on a dining table. Very tiny blooms are usually best made into a little nosegay, with just a little green foliage added if desired, and stood in a delicate wine glass or a small cup and saucer.

Violets with their faint but sweet fragrance can be packed densely into a shallow dish as they have very short stems. They can also be bunched together in an assortment of small glass jam-jars, themselves grouped within a basket. Any gaps between the jars can be covered with a little moss for an arrangement echoing the natural surroundings of the flowers.

ABOVE: Exquisite roses look
particularly effective arranged in a set
of delicate tumblers.

RIGHT: Tiny flowers need miniature
treatments. This posy of violets has
been tied with the finest ribbon.

A SELECTION OF SHRUBS

$\mathcal{O}$ ne of the real pleasures of having your own garden is to be able to grow and pick flowers that are rarely seen for sale. Many shrubs produce blossoms suitable for cutting, including mahonia, viburnum, broom, forsythia, prunus, azalea, magnolia, ceanothus and hydrangea.

Hydrangeas are very useful as floral decorations, either fresh or dried. There are several different varieties, but the commonest, the mop-head or hortensia, is also the one most often used for drying. Ranging as they do in the fresh state from white through pink and red to mauve and blue, the enormous, blowsy heads take on strange tints in the autumn, some flowers turning a bronze colour, others green, still others a metallic purple and plum.

The flowers are not dried in the usual way but picked when the petals, or bracts, start to turn crisp. The stems are stood in a small amount of water, which is slowly absorbed into the tissues. By the time the water has gone the flower-heads will be quite dry and papery.

Dried hydrangea heads massed together in baskets make wonderful winter decorations, especially in grand rooms, where few other dried flowers will have quite their impact. For smaller arrangements the heads can be split into separate florets and wired on to false stems.

Some of the most rewarding shrubs to plant are those that blossom on bare stems during the winter months. The flowers are often insignificant but the scents are spectacular. Worth searching out are the shrubby honeysuckle *Lonicera purpusii* and the winter sweet *Chimonanthus praecox*.

B ig, bold, mop-headed hydrangeas make a stunning table display. Picked later in the year, after turning rich, deep colours, they can be successfully dried for winter decorations.

A PACKETFUL
OF FLOWERS

*I*f you grow a packet or two of flower seeds you may find them such a success that day after day you will have rich pickings from the flowerbeds. Easy annuals such as cornflowers bloom right through the summer, and if you make sure to pick them regularly they will keep producing more. Once you neglect them and the first flowers set seed, however, the plants will let up, thinking they have done all they need to. So keep picking, and dry any surplus blooms for pot pourris or dried flower arrangements.

Cornflowers can be sown in the autumn for very early summer flowering, or from spring to around June for a later crop. Other good and easy hardy annuals include sweet peas, Oriental poppies, larkspur, marigolds, love-in-a-mist, lavatera, godetia and nasturtiums.

Half-hardy annuals, many of which can be bought as boxes of young plants, need to be started very early in the spring with some heat, then progressively hardened off for planting outdoors. Good ones to include in a cutting garden are nicotiana, asters, zinnias and cosmea.

There are also some biennial varieties, easily grown from seed, that make superb cut flowers. From a sowing one summer you will have blooms the next. This group includes foxgloves, Canterbury bells, sweet-williams and forget-me-nots.

Once you have a regular supply of these flowers for picking, mass them loosely around the house in an assortment of simple, wide-necked jugs.

RIGHT: Cornflowers are excellent value in a garden, flowering for months and producing a new flush of blooms after every picking.

FAR RIGHT: With a mass of asters, pinks, roses, cornflowers and sweet peas such as this, an informal arrangement in a simple, unobtrusive jug is perhaps the most pleasing.

COLOUR SCHEMING

*T*he statement that colours do not clash in nature is often used by gardeners to excuse some horrendous colour scheme in a flower border, and while there is some truth in the saying, there are certainly good colour mixes and bad ones. Peoples' perception of colour varies enormously, so there cannot really be any hard-and-fast rules when it comes to decorating with flowers.

Most flowers have inherently beautiful, often very subtle, colours, though there are exceptions to the case, usually where man has stepped in and tried to improve on nature. Successful flower arrangements can be made using just one colour, sometimes even without any green for relief. Two colours or perhaps three, but all close in tone, can also look lovely – pink, mauve and pale blue are good examples – while hot mixtures of, say, vivid scarlet, shocking pink and fuchsia sound extraordinary but can look stunning.

Another possibility is a complete mix of colours rather like that in a herbaceous border, with blues, reds, yellows and purples. This can work, too, but usually needs a touch of green to tone down and break up the very strong blocks of colour.

An all-white or all-cream arrangement is classic and elegant, though again it will need some green in it to offset the flowers. This can either be a bright, fairly acid green or a soft, blue-grey green from foliage such as rue or eucalyptus.

FAR LEFT: This cool, all-white arrangement includes lilies, tobacco flowers and foxgloves.

TOP LEFT: In this harmonious arrangement, roses, lilies, asters and stock have been grouped in a contrasting Wedgewood vase.

BOTTOM LEFT: This basket has been filled with scabious, honeysuckle, dill flowers and white daisies.

CHOOSING CONTAINERS

The containers in which you choose to put your flowers need to relate to the blooms in several ways: the material from which they are made should suit the style and colour of the flowers; their size should be right for the amount of flowers being used; and the proportions of flower to container should be as sympathetic as possible.

Baskets are available in an enormous range of shapes, textures and sizes, and are useful for fresh and dried arrangements alike. They can easily be lined with something waterproof, or can simply be used as cache-pots to hide another container. And of course they look equally perfect with country flowers and more sophisticated, exotic blooms.

A few simple, plain glass vases are extremely handy when you have just a few stems, or when you need to make a dense mass of one variety with all the stems cut to one length. Glass containers can have clear marbles or smooth, small pebbles laid inside to help support the stems, while a tiny drop of bleach can help to keep the water clear.

China vases, old and new, are good to have for more formal arrangements, and there are many other materials on offer, such as metal and plastic. Whatever your preference, remember that a container with a strong personality of its own will generally be harder to use than a more modest one, so it may be wise to invest in a few very basic vases, which, though they may not be exciting on their own, always make the flowers look superb.

LEFT: Dazzling, unsophisticated marigolds spill simply out of a classic fifties vase in a deeper burnt orange.

RIGHT: A dark-toned rustic basket is the perfect choice for this exuberant mix of golden-yellow and orange lilies, marigolds and fluffy, lime-green sprays of *Alchemilla mollis*.

THE SWEETEST FLOWER

*T*he sweet pea (*Lathyrus odoratus*) is a hardy annual that is always worth growing. Planted in the autumn or winter it will flower from very early in the summer, while from a spring sowing it will produce flowers all season long. If you keep picking, the blooms will probably continue on to the first frosts. There are dozens of varieties to choose from, all with that wonderful, luminous quality of colour, ranging from white and cream through all shades of pink and salmon, red, mauve, crimson and scarlet.

You can grow mixed colours for lovely country jugfuls or keep to more restrained and subtle arrangements of one colour. A large glass bowl of scented, cream sweet peas is a beautiful treat, as is for that matter a bowl of pink or crimson. They do mix with other flowers but somehow their beauty is best displayed when they are used alone, either in a thick, quickly arranged bunch or more formally, in a special sweet-pea bowl with space between each bloom. Sweet-pea bowls are shallow, with a perforated section inside, each hole of which is able to hold a single stem. This way of displaying sweet peas does enhance the delicacy of the petals, seen at their best with light shining through from behind.

Grow some of the traditional varieties on offer now that have the true old-fashioned fragrance. The blooms are on the small side, but the tonal range is interesting, and some have frilled edges and double colours, too.

*F*AR LEFT: The quintessential summer flower must be the sweet pea, with its lovely mix of colours.

*B*ELOW: There is little point in making a formal arrangement out of a generous bunch of sweet peas.

THE IMPORTANCE OF TEXTURE

*O*ne way of achieving dramatic and colourful results with flowers is to use very short-stemmed blooms, densely packed into shallow containers. These make a marvellous surface of colour and texture where the outline of individual flowers becomes of secondary importance, the flower-heads building up together to create a tapestry effect. To make this method work well you will need some floral foam to push the stems into. You will then be able to choose exactly where to put each flower and ensure that it is held firmly in place.

The new generation of foam absorbs water very quickly and can be cut and squeezed into virtually any container. Small, shallow baskets are perfect for this type of arrangement, but remember to line them with plastic or metal foil first: the foam may not be dripping wet to start with, but water will get pushed out as you insert the flower stems.

While your flower arrangement can be fairly casual, you can also aim for a more stylised design, for example using alternate rows of single colours or concentric circles of colour in a round basket. A centre of pink rosebuds surrounded by rings of forget-me-nots and lily-of-the-valley would make a charming Victorian Valentine picture, or you could use a random colour mix with flowers of the same variety, such as zinnias or freesias.

Whatever effect you opt for, the important thing is to begin with all your flowers cut short to the right length; the rest will follow quite simply on from there.

*S*trong-shaped flowers such as lilies and gerbera make enormous impact when arranged into a solid block of colour and texture, with no stems and little foliage showing.

WORKING WITH DRIED FLOWERS

*M*any of the things you need to know about decorating with fresh flowers also apply to dried ones, but there are a few very basic differences. Dried flowers are dead flowers, which means firstly that their petals do not have the translucency and colour of fresh ones, and secondly that they are completely stiff and still. Fresh flowers, even after cutting, may continue to open and unfurl, and sometimes grow, in water. Occasionally they will even turn to the light. Dried flowers are static and unyielding, and once they are put somewhere they stay there.

The colours in dried blooms are often very subtle and rich, and overall the flowers have wonderful textures and sometimes quite sculptural shapes. But they do slowly lose their hue, and usually by the time most of their colour has gone they are also old, tired, dusty and in need of replacement. Standing dried flowers in a strong source of light is not a good idea, as it simply hastens this fading process.

Perfect for putting in dark or overheated rooms, however, they are the answer for people who love flowers in the house but cannot always manage to have fresh ones. They seem to look best when they are used in strong, uncluttered arrangements, and when they are thickly packed and full of texture. Very wispy, grassy mixtures can look insipid, and too many of them in one house tend to appear boring and fussy. Take your colour scheme from furnishings or decorations and aim for simplicity. A pretty basket filled with just one type of dried flower, such as lavender or hydrangea, can have enormous impact and a great sense of style.

When new, dried flowers have almost the same richness of colour as their fresh counterparts. They should always be thickly massed for maximum impact, in containers sympathetic to their special qualities.

TECHNIQUES AND MATERIALS

*M*ost dried flowers used in arrangements retain their own stems, but occasionally you will need to put a wire on a flower-head if, for example, it has been dried without its stem in a desiccant. Stub wires, as they are known, are easy to buy and come in various thicknesses. One flower that always needs an artificial stem is helichrysum, and the best way to attach this is when the flower is fresh, so that the wire rusts into the head as it dries. If you try putting the wire in later it will go in with great difficulty and will not stay in place quite as firmly.

Almost without exception you will need floral foam for dried flower arrangements. Certain swags and garlands are built on straw bases, but generally baskets and other containers need to be filled with the dry, beigey-brown foam sold specially for this purpose. It can be cut in the same way as the wet type and taped into position if you need to secure it. Aim to cover it completely or at least not to be able to see it through any gaps. If you cannot avoid these, you can always fill them in at the end with dried lichen, moss or small flower-heads.

Often it is expensive or extravagant to use too many of the more glamorous flowers in one arrangement, so you can supplement them with filler material, which is bulky and makes a good background, rather as you might use foliage in a fresh arrangement. Examples of fillers are *Alchemilla mollis* and sea lavender.

Jars of glowing, freshly dried
helichrysums, each flower-head fixed
to a stiff wire stem after picking, make
a bold mantelpiece decoration that
will last for many months.

POTTED DECORATIONS

Growing flowers in pots to bring indoors seems a sensible idea well worth copying. Many summer-flowering plants such as fuchsias, while not enjoying living permanently in a house, are very happy inside for the odd week or two when they are in flower.

One of the best of all plants to grow for this treatment is the lily. Planted into sandy compost in pots in early spring and left outdoors to develop naturally, it can be brought indoors as it opens from July onwards. Choose varieties that are highly scented and be generous with your planting. Odd numbers of bulbs always seem to look best, so aim for pots of at least three and preferably five or seven. After they have flowered, liquid-feed them and put them back outside to die down. They should come back year after year.

Little pots of topiary contrived from clipped box or tiny herb plants make old-fashioned and rather charming decorations, particularly if they are used in pairs. Try making a miniature rose tree from a ball of wet foam on a stem, stuck into more foam inside a small terracotta pot. Put sprigs of a small-leaved evergreen all over the ball to make a dense, mop-headed tree. Finish off with several small rosebuds or a few tiny spray roses.

LEFT: This miniature potted tree has been made from tiny evergreen leaves and rosebuds pressed into a damp foam ball. The old terracotta pot is just the right container.

RIGHT: Any variety of lily can be grown in pots outdoors and brought indoors for flowering. These glorious yellow lilies are at their best and ready to be moved inside.

INDOOR GARDENING

*T*he popularity of flowering pot plants as home decorations continues to grow. Many of them are quite short lived but will still last longer than most cut flowers. Some of the best and most spectacular varieties, such as azaleas and cyclamen, are available through the winter months, though both these plants can be slightly tricky to maintain unless you have just the right conditions.

The beautifully scented, white-flowered jasmine, often seen growing indoors, is a good, long-term pot plant that can be trained and pruned to the shape and size you want. Small pots of flowers such as African violets (saintpaulias) or primroses always look best and make greatest impact if they are grouped together in fives or sixes, perhaps in a larger container such as a basket.

One of the most satisfying ways of providing flowers for the house is to plant some of the vast range of flowering bulbs on offer. However, you must be organised enough to plant them well ahead in order to give them the period of dormancy, then growth, that they need before flowering. Hyacinths and some narcissi can be planted in early autumn to flower at Christmas, or you can simply plant bulbs through the autumn and have a succession of flowering pots right through from winter to spring. If you want very early-flowering bulbs, be sure to buy those that have been specially prepared for this purpose. Try planting some of the miniature irises, as well as the early-flowering winter crocus. Species tulips are successful, too, as well as less commonly pot-grown bulbs such as grape hyacinths and scillas.

RIGHT: Miniature golden narcissi in a pot greet the spring cheerfully, and a few weeks earlier than those outside.

FAR RIGHT: Jasmine can be trained into a standard plant within a couple of years. A pair together look perfect.

ALL ABOUT GARLANDS

The circle is a satisfying and beautiful shape, carrying with it a wealth of symbolic meaning to do with its unbroken line and continuity. The making of circular garlands from flowers or other plant material seems to have a long European and American history, but not one particularly in Great Britain. Evergreen garlands are hung on doors as a welcome at Christmas, but wreaths of flowers are not seen very often.

Garlands have an unsophisticated feel that is very appealing, and however clumsy you may be at putting flowers together, with a circle you cannot seem to go wrong. The base with which you start is important, as is the size of the flowers in relation to it.

You can buy floral foam rings for both wet and dry arrangements, and these make garland construction very simple. Alternatively, you can make your own base, either from straw or from wire and moss: Christmas evergreen garlands are traditionally made up on rings of wet moss and wire, but you do need a good eye and deft fingers to make these; a straw base is perfect for dried flowers, but again it can be rather fiddly to make, and straw is not the easiest commodity to find if you live in a town. The advantage of making your own base is that it can be any size you like, and also that you can use many different types of plant material on it. A purchased foam base, on the other hand, needs to be very thickly covered so as not to show through, and this may limit the type and shape of flowers used.

Left: The flaming colours of this striking autumn garland derive from its mix of dahlias, gerbera and sedum, spiced up with the warm red tones of glossy rose-hips.

Cool and sophisticated, this fragile-looking garland uses a combination of white gladioli flowers, dill and variegated foliage in shades of cream and green to create a serene effect.

GARLANDS
FRESH AND DRY

Whether you are putting together a fresh flower garland or a dry one, the process is really very similar. Try out your first examples of both on a floral foam base, which is a quick and easy way of getting a superb effect. Soak the foam beforehand if you are using fresh flowers, and ensure that you have enough plant material for the size of base you are using: the flowers will need to be densely packed to hide all the foam. If the garland is to hang on a vertical surface rather than lie flat on a table, work with it hanging in front of you. Cut all the stems of flowers and foliage very short to keep everything just above the surface of the foam, otherwise the garland will look top heavy and clumsy.

To start with, use a filler material or a flower or foliage you have plenty of and put this in place. Work around the garland evenly, remembering to cover the inside and outside edges of the ring. Next, put in any special flowers or large bits of material, spacing them carefully to give a well-balanced look (garlands seem to work best arranged in a regular way, though a completely random mix

would look good if you had masses of totally different flowers and colours). If you have any small flowers, use them in little bunches or groups, so that they do not become lost in the arrangement and are able to hold their own with the larger blooms. Finish off with all the middle-sized material remaining.

If you intend to hang the garland on a wall or door, remember to provide it with a loop. Make this from a piece of wire or string tied around the base and hidden among the flowers. An extra touch is to attach a pretty ribbon or bow to the garland, but keep it simple and subtle and let the flowers speak for themselves.

RIGHT: This harvest wreath has been made from ripe ears of wheat, poppies, cornflowers and chamomile.

BELOW: Densely packed achillea, dill flowers and tiny orange rose-hips make a soft, late-summer garland.

SWAGS AND ROPES

*I*t is difficult sometimes to give dried flower arrangements the natural and spontaneous appearance possible with fresh blooms. One way of achieving some movement and softness is to make a rope or swag of dried flowers for use along a piece of furniture or mantelpiece, or around a picture frame, clock or mirror. For special occasions festoons of this kind look wonderful twining down a staircase or looped over a door frame.

Making a long length of flowered rope is very time consuming and requires a large number of flowers, but it is not too difficult. Begin with thick string or soft rope as a base to build on. Next, make lots of small bunches of flowers or a filler material and wire each one tightly, leaving an end of wire free. Fix each of these bunches to the rope, working in one direction all the time and overlapping bunch upon bunch. You should finish up with a thick, flower-covered rope that will drape and curve easily.

A simpler and less stylised method is to find stems of tall climbers such as hops or wild clematis and to use these as natural swags. Secure them with tiny pins or tacks and add a few extra flowers or pieces of foliage to fill them out and make a pretty shape. Use very fine rose wire to attach these flowers to the natural stem.

To decorate a frame or mirror, try to make the rope a single entity that can simply be draped over the object, or fixed, if necessary, with the minimum of pins or tape. Make use of any irregularities or holes there may be in the frame to attach the plant material.

Left and below: Some plants grow in long swags ideal for decorating with. Here, dried hops, along with tiny red rosebuds and hips, have been used to dress up a cottage mantelpiece.

FLOWERS ON THE FLAT

*P*ressing flowers between sheets of absorbent paper results in another version of the dried product, but this is obviously a two-dimensional version, lacking any structure or solidity, which can be used only to make flat decorations and pictures.

To begin with, choose perfect blooms that are not too bulky. Lay each flower on a sheet of absorbent cartridge or blotting paper placed on a piece of stiff card. Leave plenty of space around each bloom. Lay another sheet of absorbent paper carefully over the flowers and then another piece of card over this. The whole sandwich can now be put into a flower press, if you have one, or laid on a flat surface and weighed down with large books or any other flat, heavy objects. The time taken to press the flowers thoroughly will depend on the varieties you have used, and will be anything from three or four days to several weeks. To check how they are pressing, gently lift one corner and look, but be careful not to disturb the whole page or tear off any delicate petals. When the flowers are ready they can be lifted off the paper with a sharp-bladed knife and used for making pictures or anything else that comes to mind.

As well as pressing flowers, always do a few pretty leaves and ferns as well, choosing plant material with a good silhouette that can be used as a foil for the flowers. Bear in mind also the durability of the colours concerned. Some flower colours are very fleeting, while others, like blue and carmine, seem quite permanent. But even if the colours do fade, the shapes and textures of pressed flowers are every bit as exciting as those of fresh blooms, and often more so.

*R*IGHT: Pressed flowers made into a simple picture are shown off to perfection in an antique frame.

*B*ELOW: Fresh flowers may be pressed all through the summer and set aside for use in the winter months.

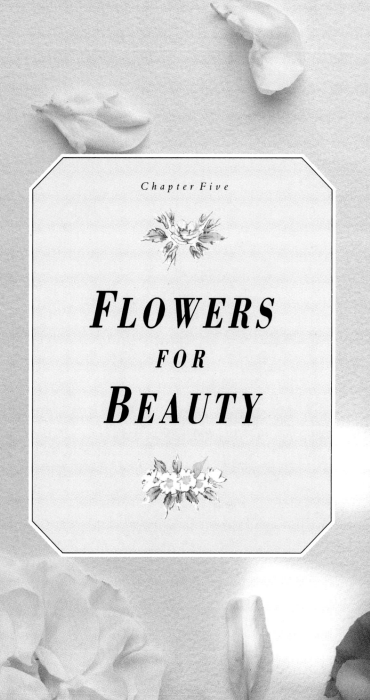

Chapter Five

FLOWERS
FOR
BEAUTY

There is a long tradition of using flowers for beauty. Alongside their usefulness as medicines, flowers, leaves and herbs were long ago discovered to have all kinds of beneficial qualities when steeped in various lotions and creams, or simply made for use as infusions. Through the centuries, flowers were found to contain qualities that soothed and softened skin, brightened and strengthened hair, or simply relaxed and scented a tired body in a deliciously fragrant bath.

We never seem to grow tired of flower scents in the beauty preparations we use, and nowadays, more than ever before, feel a need for simple and straight-forward products that are as far removed as possible from the chemist's laboratory. There are many simple and natural things to make at home. Start with an infusion of flowers for a facial steam or make some scented bath bags. Once you have tried a recipe, adapt and alter it to suit your taste, and remember that all these beauty ideas make stunning gifts.

SCENTED STEAM

*A*ny skin that has to put up with city grime and pollution welcomes the occasional thorough cleansing over a scented steam bath. The heat and humidity open up its pores and leave it ready for a follow-up toning. You can use fresh or dried flower petals and herbs, a single fragrance or a mix of several. Traditionally, lime flowers, marigolds and elderflowers were used for their beneficial qualities, but it is also good to use a strongly scented bath of rose petals on their own.

ROSE-PETAL FACIAL STEAM

1¾ pints (1 litre) pure water (bottled mineral water is best)
Approx. 5 tablespoons fresh, strongly scented rose petals
2 or 3 drops rose essential oil

Heat the water to boiling. Put the petals in a large bowl and pour the water over them. Add the oil, stir well, and leave for 3 minutes.

To use the facial steam, first thoroughly cleanse your face with your favourite method. Hold your face over the bowl, but not too close to the water, and cover your head with a towel. Try to remain over the steam for about 10 minutes if you can, but take a breather every now and again. Finish off with a cooling down, using plain, lukewarm water, and do not rush outside straight away into the cold air. Instead, let your skin gradually return to a normal temperature, pat it dry, and finish off with a gentle, refreshing toner such as the rose-petal water described on page 123.

For a more astringent version of the facial steam, try using rosemary, fresh or dried, as well as peppermint and sage. Aim for a once-weekly steam: this will keep your face really clean and unclogged, and will be a perfect form of enforced relaxation, too.

L*EFT: Pure luxury and ten minutes' enforced rest come with this sweetly scented, rose-petal facial steam.*

F*or all infusions, choose rose petals with a strong perfume, and pick them on a dry day.*

FEET FIRST

$\mathcal{F}$eet are very often the most neglected part of a skin-care routine, yet they repay all the attention given to them. A quick, effective pick-me-up for tired, aching feet is a foot bath infused with fragrant flowers. Try using lavender, peppermint and rosemary.

LAVENDER AND MINT FOOT BATH

3½ pints (2 litres) pure water (bottled mineral water is best)
3 stems fresh peppermint or 1 tablespoon dried
6 flowering stems lavender or 2 tablespoons dried flowers
1 or 2 drops lavender essential oil

Heat 10 fl oz (300 ml) of the water to boiling point and pour over the flowers in a small bowl or jug. Leave to infuse for at least 15 minutes, then strain into a large bowl. Add the oil, stir well and top up with the rest of the water at a comfortably hot temperature. Soak your feet for 15 minutes or so, and when you have finished pat them dry and rub in a lotion or oil to soften them.

Almond oil can be infused with peppermint, lavender, marigold or lime flowers and used for an after-bath foot massage. Buy sweet almond oil from a chemist and add as many flower petals as possible. Leave the mixture in a screwtop jar in a warm, sunny place such as a windowsill for about 3 weeks, then gently heat in a small saucepan until the petals appear to crispen and cook. Carefully strain the oil from the petals and pour into bottles, adding a fresh flower sprig to each if desired.

RIGHT: A lavender and peppermint foot bath, here infusing before use, is a wonderful refresher for aching feet.

BELOW: Lavender has been used in cosmetics for many centuries, chiefly for its pungent, long-lasting scent.

BOTTLED SCENTS

*R*efreshing, mild skin toners and lotions are easily made from flower petals, and so are hair rinses and even shampoos. If making your own shampoo sounds too difficult, a simple after-wash rinse will naturally correct the acid/alkaline balance of your hair, and make it smell wonderful, too.

ROSE-PETAL WATER

A very mild toner can be made from roses, and it is perfect for softening and refreshing the skin after cleansing, without being harsh. Whilst it is better to leave the making of true rose water to the professionals, who use tons of roses and complicated distillation processes, it is very simple to prepare a rose-scented water. Start with any strongly scented rose petals, preferably from one of the old-fashioned varieties. *Rosa officinalis* was

traditionally cultivated for the perfume industry, and it is worth growing a bush of it for its abundant, scented crimson flowers.

Douse a jarful of rose petals with boiling water and add vodka in the proportion of 1 part spirits to 10 parts water (it is not always easy to buy medicinal alcohol, which has no smell, so vodka makes a very good substitute in recipes such as these). Cover and leave to infuse. When cool, strain off the liquid and pour into sterilised bottles. Add a fresh petal or two to each bottle as a pretty finishing touch. Use as a mild skin freshener or toner, or add to a bath.

CHAMOMILE HAIR RINSE

Hair rinses can be infused with many different herbs and flowers according to your hair type and colour. Chamomile has long been used for its slight lightening qualities on blonde hair, but for brown hair substitute sage, rosemary or marigold for a darker sheen.

Boil 18 fl oz (500 ml) of distilled or pure water. Add 4 tablespoons of fresh chamomile flower-heads or 2 tablespoons of dried. Take off the heat and leave to infuse. Add 2 tablespoons of distilled vinegar and allow to cool. Strain and store in sterilised bottles. After shampooing the hair pour over it 6 tablespoons of the hair rinse mixed with half a litre of warm water.

T*op left*: Home-made rose-petal water deserves to be stored in a pretty glass bottle. With a petal or two floating inside and a label attached, it makes a charming present.

F*ar left*: When used regularly, shampoos, conditioners and rinses infused with chamomile are said to lighten the colour of mousy or fair hair, and also to brighten its shine.

BAGS OF LUXURY

*M*any bath preparations these days contain harsh detergents and artificial scents, and are often far from soothing and softening, as they claim to be. If you make your own bath sachets filled with the ingredients of your choice, you will have wonderful, scented baths that will leave your skin refreshed but not dry.

If sewing the bags does not appeal you can make them very easily without having to pick up a needle. Simply cut a square of muslin, cheesecloth or any other gauzy fabric and put a spoonful of the ingredients (see recipe) in the middle. Tie round the top with string, ribbon or thread and you will have a bath sachet. Bath bags are nothing more than strips of the same fabric measuring about 13 inches (33 cm) long by 3 inches (8 cm) wide, folded in half and sewn down the two sides. Once they have been turned inside out and filled, pink the top edges or else leave them raw. Tie the neck with string or strong thread. A small box or basket filled with these bags makes a lovely present. They can be hung under a flowing tap or dropped straight into the water, and should last for at least two baths. Choose sweet and flowery scents or spicy and astringent ones, according to your taste.

The recipe below is for a basic mixture, which can be adapted and added to at will, depending on the result you want. The bran, oatmeal and dried milk, as well as providing bulk, act as water softeners, making the bath smooth and silky. The colour is not important but the fragrance of the ingredients is, if you want good results.

BASIC BATH-BAG MIXTURE

1 cup wheat bran
1 cup oatmeal
½ cup dried milk powder
1 cup dried, highly scented rose petals
1 cup dried lavender flowers
½ cup lemon-verbena leaves (or rosemary)

Mix all the ingredients together in a large bowl and spoon into sachets. Keep any surplus in a screwtop jar and use as required.

For an exotic, luxurious version use some dried jasmine flowers in the mixture.

L<small>EFT</small>: Bath bags may either be dropped straight into the water or tied to the tap of a basin or bath.

R<small>IGHT</small>: Small muslin bags filled with flowers and other ingredients soften and scent bathwater in a natural way.

Chapter Six

FLOWERS
FOR
SPECIAL
OCCASIONS

Weddings, birthdays, anniversaries, celebrations and parties: none of these special events would be quite right without flowers, whether used to make decorations or bouquets, or else combined with other ingredients to make lasting floral gifts. Flowers always seem to strike the right note, no matter what the occasion, cheering someone who is feeling low, or saying 'thank you' more eloquently than any words could do. A house decorated with a vase or two of fragrant blooms is warm and welcoming, and with a few extra touches flowers can create a sparkling atmosphere for any party.

In this chapter you will find dozens of ideas for using flowers in ways that are a bit special, whether it be a carefully hand-covered box filled with home-made pot pourri to give to a favourite friend, or a simple but sophisticated wedding bouquet for a summer bride. There are some old-fashioned ideas well worth reviving, such as lavender bottles based on those made centuries ago, before the days of air fresheners and insecticides, and used for refreshing linen. There are pretty Victorian-style posies to give as presents or to complement a dress, and other ideas for using flowers imaginatively, from turning a simple straw hat into a stunning wedding eye-catcher to making fragrant ink and writing paper for romantic letter-writing. From a single rose stem to a houseful of arrangements, flowers always have their own sense of occasion.

CANDLES AND FLOWERS

𝒫arties and special occasions call out for special decorations, but this need not mean that they have to be lavish, expensive and difficult to make. The most effective results usually come from a simple idea well executed. Candles add sparkle and fun to any party, and combined with flowers make spectacular table centrepieces or room decorations.

It is possible to buy small, colourful candles designed to be floated in water, but ordinary white night-lights can also be used and are every bit as effective. A group of these floated in a shallow container will look stunning, and for even more drama small flower-heads or petals can be dropped in among them. A glass dish gives maximum sparkle and a mirror backdrop doubles the effect instantly. If you prefer, you can colour the water subtly with food colourings, and even scent it with a few drops of a flower essential oil. Stand a decoration like this on a buffet table or put several on low surfaces around a large room.

Tall, thin candles, too, are often used among flowers, which is fine as long as you remember to keep a strict eye on them as they burn down. Try standing a group of them in a container of water (you can support them with small lumps of plasticine or florists' putty) and floating flowers or petals around their base.

Fᴀʀ ʟᴇꜰᴛ: Bowlfuls of floating candles mixed with petals or flowers – golden-yellow chrysanthemums in this case – can be used as table decorations, or to enliven party settings.

Lᴇꜰᴛ: A mass of scented petals floating in water has been used to decorate this tin jelly mould, and at the same time to hide the florists' putty supporting the candles.

PACKAGED SCENTS

*I*f you have prepared a batch of home-made pot pourri it is satisfying to be able to put it to its various uses, and not just to have it lying about in containers. Blends of herbs and flowers meant to relax and to promote sleep can be put into special pillows, and a scoop or two of any scented pot pourri works wonders sewn into a padded hanger or shoe shaper.

The most practical way to scent a cushion is to put the mixture into a small bag, which is then tucked into an external pocket or hidden inside the cover. Here it can be replenished or changed whenever necessary. The bag can be filled entirely with pot pourri, or made from a combination of soft wadding and pot pourri. The wadding makes for a good, squashy shape and encases the mixture, preventing it from escaping via the seams.

A pretty floral cushion complete with pocket and sachet makes a superb gift. Choose a flowery print and try perhaps to match it with an appropriate scent, so that, for example, a rose-strewn fabric will smell deliciously of summer roses. If you make the sachet to slip inside the cover, keep it flat so that it will not pull the cushion out of shape.

Scented sachets can also be added to hot-water-bottle covers. Make the cover from a piece of ready-quilted fabric and add a pocket in the shape of a basket over a bunch of appliquéd flowers. Tuck a flower-shaped sachet into the pocket.

FAR LEFT: A scented sachet is kept in a pocket sewn on to one side of this pretty cushion.

TOP LEFT: This pretty cover for a hot-water bottle has a sachet tucked into its appliquéd pocket.

BOTTOM LEFT: Here, a large, flamboyant bow has been used to anchor the sachet to the cushion.

SCENTED
TEA-TIMES

scented tea cosy is a wonderfully old-fashioned idea, one well worth adopting even in the day of the tea-bag. You can either make a padded cover with pot pourri sewn in with the wadding or, for a more practical result, a separate bag or sachet (based on the pattern described on page 137) slotted into a pocket or tucked into a band inside the cosy.

To make things even simpler it is possible to buy ready-padded and -quilted fabrics, but the choice of designs in these is admittedly rather limited. A better idea is to pick a piece of ordinary material, line it with a matching, related or contrasting fabric, and finally pad it with polyester wadding. Alternatively, it is sometimes possible to find an attractive tea cosy second-hand and to adapt this. A plain linen one with a decoration of cutwork, for example, could be lined with a strong, plain-coloured fabric and a scent sachet put into a pocket in the lining.

The flower mixture used in the sachet can be fresh and summery or warm and spicy, according to your taste and the tea you serve. Try a lemon-scented sachet for a fresh, clean smell perfect for a summer tea-time in the garden, or use one with a high proportion of spicy smells, such as cinnamon and nutmeg, for a traditional winter's tea of warm scones and rich fruit cake. Whatever mixture you choose, you will find that the warmth from the brewing tea will gently release the scent, filling the air with delicious fragrance.

RIGHT: The warmth from a brewing pot of tea brings out the scent of flowers from a sachet on the cosy.

FAR RIGHT: Crisp white linen and a deep-blue fabric have been used for this tea cosy, which contains an internal pocket for a scented sachet.

LAVENDER BOTTLES

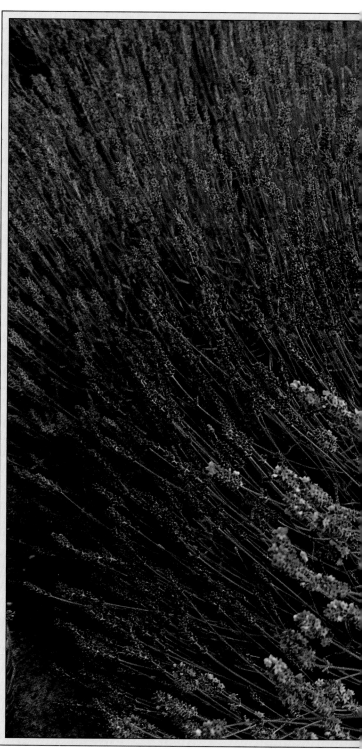

*L*avender has ever been the traditional wash-day herb. White cotton or linen sheets and clothes, left to bleach in the sun, have been draped over billowing bushes of lavender in countless old-fashioned gardens, while the dried flower-heads, left on their stems or rubbed off into sachets, have always been used to scent and keep linens fresh in storage. The smell of lavender, while clean and slightly antiseptic, is also warm and appealing, and it must be one of the best known and loved of all scents, whether used alone or added to perfume mixtures alongside other ingredients.

There are several varieties that you can grow and, though the dark, purple-flowered types are pretty, the best scent comes from the larger-growing Old English lavender, which blooms later in the summer on long stems and is very strongly perfumed. It is the perfect choice for lavender bottles, which have long been used to scent drawers and cupboards and are so called because they encase the flower-heads and so stop the flowers from dropping off into the linen.

To make one bottle you will need about 20 stems of lavender fully opened and freshly picked. Tie a thin piece of thread around the base of the flower-heads and bend each stem back in turn, encasing the flowers. When they are all bent back, arrange them neatly and tie again with string or ribbon just beneath the enclosed flowers, latticing in and out of the stems if desired. Leave the bottle to dry naturally, then use as desired.

*L*avender bottles have been used for centuries to keep stored linen and clothes fresh and sweet. Their clever construction ensures that the flowers do not drop off once they are dry.

SWEET BAGS AND SACHETS

The simplest sweet bag to make, one that needs no sewing at all, consists of a square, lace-edged handkerchief filled with a scoop of pot pourri, tied with a piece of ribbon and finished off with a bow. Following on from this are all kinds of small sachets and bags filled with pot pourri or mixtures of this with wadding. If using new fabrics choose carefully, bearing in mind where the sachets will be used. Sweet bags used for sheets and bedding look good in crisp stripes, fresh colours and no-nonsense designs, while those placed among underwear and delicate clothes can be made from satin, lace and snippets of silk.

A basic sweet bag is made from a strip of fabric about 19 inches (48 cm) long by 4 inches (10 cm) wide. Right sides together, fold the strip in half and narrow-seam up both sides. Turn it right way out and tuck the top 3¼ inches (8 cm) down inside the bag. Fill it with pot pourri, or a mixture of wadding and pot pourri, and tie with a ribbon tightly around the neck. Lace edgings, initials, machine embroidery and any other decorative touches can all be added before the bag has been filled. One word of advice: the pot pourri should not be too lumpy or contain any large pieces, otherwise it will spoil the shape of the bag. A good recipe for general use is below.

SWEET-BAG RECIPE

1 cup strongly scented rose petals
1 cup lavender
½ cup lemon-verbena leaves
½ cup crushed rosemary
¼ cup powdered orris root
2 crushed cinnamon sticks
Few drops rose essential oil

Mix the dry ingredients together in a large bowl. Add drops of oil until the scent is right. Put the mixture in a paper bag, shake, seal loosely and leave in a dark place for 2 weeks. Use to fill sachets and bags as required.

LEFT AND BELOW: Sweet-scented bags and sachets can be made in all shapes and sizes, but for a quick result, a pretty handkerchief is best.

KEEPING
MOTHS AWAY

Above: An old Paisley shawl makes
the perfect soft fabric for use in sewing
scented sachets for clothes-hangers.

Far right: Nosegays of moth-
repellent plants are often far too pretty
to be kept hanging in a cupboard.

Dried and fresh herbs and flowers have been used over the centuries for all manner of household purposes, but keeping harmful insects away from fabrics and other susceptible items in storage has always been particularly important. Plants used to combat these indoor pests have traditionally included southernwood, pennyroyal, tansy and rue.

If you do not like the idea of modern insecticides, try hanging a few small bagfuls of these plants among your clothes, or slipping the odd sachetful in between your knitwear during the summer. Even simpler to make, small bunches of herbs and flowers hung in wardrobes and cupboards are pretty enough to use as decorations in their own right, on the back of a bedroom door, above a bedhead, or against a good-looking piece of furniture.

Moth bags are made in the same way as sweet bags (page 137), but the recipe for the filling differs slightly in that it contains a few special herbs.

RECIPE FOR MOTH BAGS AND SACHETS

1 cup dried lavender flowers
1 cup dried, crumbled southernwood
½ cup dried, crumbled rosemary
½ cup dried, crumbled tansy leaves (optional)
4 teaspoons powdered orris root

Combine all the ingredients and put into suitable bags and sachets.

To make a small bunch of herbs and flowers, choose an assortment that includes both moth-repellent plants and more decorative ones. A few whole cinnamon sticks will look good, as will a lavender bottle, if you have made one (page 134). Otherwise a few lavender stems, a sprig or two of sea lavender or *Alchemilla mollis*, some dried southernwood and sprigs of rosemary, all bunched together and tightly wired, will be very effective. Finish off with a loop made from a length of narrow velvet ribbon.

PERFECT POSIES

This soft, subtle nosegay of herb
leaves and flowers includes mint,
chicory, borage, fennel and thyme.

The pale-blue, ragged flowers of
chicory have the clear, infinite colour
of a perfect summer sky.

A posy makes the prettiest present. It is neat and portable and, once it has been admired, can be stood just as it is in a small vase or bowl. Posies are simple to put together and need no special skills, other than an eye for colour and the ability to choose compatible flower varieties.

The shape of a posy is based on the old-fashioned tussie-mussie, or small nosegay of herbs, used centuries ago to repel pungent smells and ward off disease and illness. Nowadays, whatever its purpose, a posy can be larger or smaller than its aromatic forebear, but once the stems are bunched together they should not be too bulky and should fit neatly into the hand. As to the design, this can be casual or formal, according to taste. In Victorian and Edwardian times, highly stylised and symmetrical versions were common, and these still work very well, making charming bouquets for tiny bridesmaids, for example, or beautiful gifts.

The soft, delicate colours and shapes of herb flowers combine to produce delicious little scented posies that are every bit as pretty as ones consisting entirely of decorative blooms. Do not forget to include at least one or two of the many lovely leaves to be found in the herb garden, such as variegated mint and thyme, golden marjoram, blue rue and feathery fennel and dill.

Try also to make some highly scented nosegays, using freesias, roses, lilac, hyacinths, pinks and any of the stronger-smelling blooms. People can never resist sniffing a bunch of flowers, so be sure to provide at least one or two varieties with a delicious fragrance.

FAR LEFT: A summer mixture of pale
pink, blue and mauve. The pinks are
sweetly scented and perfect for posies.

A POSY
FOR ALL SEASONS

*T*he method of making a posy is really the same whatever its size and no matter what it contains.

For a formal version, start with a single perfect flower such as a rosebud and arrange concentric bands of flowers around it, using contrasting or complementary colours and varieties for each new band. For a softer, looser effect, simply pick up a few of the flowers you have chosen and, holding them in one hand, work around the bunch, adding single flowers or little clusters until the posy is the right size. Always tie the stems with string or bind them tightly with wire, quite high up and close to the flowers. Trim them neatly and to the same length, leaving enough to make a decent handle. Cover the wire with a ribbon, if you wish, or, for a really superb finish, frame the posy with a pretty paper or fabric ruffle.

The easiest way to achieve a ruffle is to use a ready-made, circular paper doily. Cut the doily once from the outer edge into the centre. Snip a small circle out of the centre to accommodate the thickness of the stems, then wrap the doily around the posy, overlapping the cut edges so as to form a cone around the flowers. Glue, staple or pin the raw edges together. Finally, bind the stems with special waterproof tape or ribbon to keep in the moisture. This is particularly important if the posy is to be carried for any length of time, at a wedding, say, or if you simply want to keep it fresh for as long as possible.

If all this sounds rather fiddly and difficult, take heart from the fact that often the prettiest posy of all is the simple handful of buttercups or daisies gathered by a child, and none the worse for being picked in haste.

Far right: Purple lilac flowers and pink roses backed with blue combine to make a romantic Victorian posy.

White lilac and sweetly fragrant lily-of-the-valley are set off perfectly by the palest cream collar.

This richly textured posy in pink and cream includes anemones, roses both large and small, and statice.

THE BRIDE'S BOUQUET

*M*aking a wedding bouquet might seem such a daunting task that most people would not dream of attempting it at home. However, the fashion now for brides to carry soft and simple bunches or sheaves of flowers means that it is certainly possible to put together something special very easily. All that needs to be done before the big day, apart from the bouquet itself, is a little research into just what flowers are available, and in what colours. While it is possible to get many flowers out of season at a price, in general it is better to stay with those that are seasonal and at their peak.

For an informal bunch, flowers with reasonably simple shapes and fairly large heads work best. Using these you will not need too many stems, either, and the whole bouquet will stay clean and uncluttered. A filler of soft, hazy flowers such as gypsophila, or one of the small starry daisies now available, will soften and blur the general outline and blend together the stronger-shaped flowers.

The method of making a large bunch of flowers is quite similar to that used for a posy. Leave all the stems as long as possible to begin with, as they can be trimmed right at the end. Start with one or two flowers and, always holding the bunch in the same hand, add more with the other, working round more or less in a spiral so that the stems have a slight twist to them. When you have achieved a pleasing result, bind the stems about half-way down and trim the ends neatly, either straight across or with a diagonal cut. Finish the whole thing off with a ribbon, if desired.

Left: Bold, simple and very easy to make, this bridal bouquet uses the grey-green leaves of eucalyptus as a foil for an all-white mix of lilies, dill flowers and gerbera.

This glowing posy for a summer bridesmaid includes sunny lilies and chrysanthemums, offset by small white Michaelmas daisies, green poppy heads and a golden collar.

A BRIMFUL OF FLOWERS

*T*here are all kinds of occasions, summer and winter, when a hat makes an outfit extra special, providing it with a touch of flamboyance or fun. Perhaps the most useful hats to own are those that are classic and simple in shape. These can be dressed up very easily, turned into something stylish and sophisticated or else rustic and pretty just by adding a few flowers, a twist of fabric or a ribbon or two. A century ago, when they were worn on almost every occasion, hats were bought to last and added to in this way regularly, so that they would look different each time. Nowadays hats only appear at special events, so it seems to make even more sense to own one or two favourites that can be adapted at will.

Fresh flowers will last long enough for most parties and receptions, and the stems can always be wrapped to keep them moist longer. You can run a whole row of flowers around the brim, or arrange just one perfect, full-blown peony or rose at a strategic point. You can wrap a beautiful piece of fabric around the crown and use flowers that echo its colours to make a posy towards the back of the hat, or else tuck one or two flowers under the brim to peep out from below.

Dried flowers, too, look good on a hat, though they are bound to have a simple country look rather than any great sophistication. Anchor the flowers temporarily with pins, fixing them either straight into the hat or else into the hat band or ribbon, if there is one. Straw hats are perfect for this treatment and have a casual charm that goes well with most clothes.

The plainest straw hat can be transformed with the aid of a small piece of flowered fabric and a bunch of matching flowers. An unlikely colour mix of red and mauve works surprisingly well.

THE
SCENTED DESK

*P*ersonal letter-writing is on the decline, but perhaps we should revive the art and give it another dimension by adding flower scents to the papers and ink we use.

The fragrance that is chosen should be subtle and restrained, and not so powerful as to overpower the person opening the envelope. Probably the best way to add just a hint of scent is to store writing paper in a drawer containing a sweet bag or sachet. The paper will then slowly absorb the scent.

Another method is to drop a little flower essential oil on to sheets of tissue paper and layer these between sheets of writing paper. Left for a few weeks again, the fragrance will transfer itself from tissue to paper. The scent you choose will obviously depend very much on your personal taste, but any pot pourri or essential oil will give paper an unexpected and delicious smell.

Ink can be lightly scented for use in fountain pens, too. Below is a recipe for a version using the clean, citrusy scent of lemon verbena.

LEMON INK

2 oz (60 g) dried lemon-verbena leaves
½ cup water
Approx. 2½ fl oz (60 ml) bottled ink
2 drops lemon-verbena essential oil

Boil the leaves in the water in a small enamel pan until only a very little brown liquid is left. Strain, cool, and add to the ink along with the essential oil. Shake gently to mix and use as needed.

L<small>EFT</small>: Writing ink is almost as easy to scent as paper. The fragrance is best used with discretion, however, and should be fairly faint but lingering for the best results.

L<small>emon</small> verbena has a citrusy smell almost more lemony than lemons themselves, and is worth growing for its versatility in anything from food and pot pourris to sweet bags and ink.

PAPERING OVER

*P*ot pourri makes one of the nicest and most welcome presents, especially if it is a home-made version prepared from garden flowers. It deserves to be presented as attractively as possible, and not just tipped into any old bag or carton. If nothing else is to hand, at least use crisp cellophane, which looks professional and has a lovely shine. Tie the top tightly with ribbon or string and add a label describing the fragrance.

Save small boxes whenever you can for decorating. Try covering one with cut-outs from magazines and seed catalogues to build up a lovely flowery surface. This is fun to do but does take time, and the finished box needs to be coated with a layer or two of varnish to smooth over the joins and give a good gloss. A simpler way of achieving this effect is to cover a box with a piece of good-quality flowered wallpaper (wrapping paper is not as good, being rather less opaque). Either coat the wrong side of the paper with adhesive and glue it to the box, or use strips of double-sided tape. Cut a gift tag from one of the flowers in the wallpaper, punch a hole in it and loop some string through to attach to the box. Tie the box securely with string or ribbon so that there is no chance of the pot pourri being spilt.

I f you make your own pot pourri to give away, make sure to wrap and package it attractively. Here, an ordinary cardboard box has been transformed with a piece of floral wallpaper.

BOXING CLEVER

𝒫lain, undecorated wooden boxes make ideal containers for pot pourri. They can be painted or stencilled, varnished or sprayed, even left quite unadorned if preferred. A pretty effect can be obtained using small clusters of dried flowers glued into place, or instead of flowers a few dried seed-heads or pods. Poppy seed-heads are lovely left their natural, sculptured greyish green, but they can also look quite splendid painted a dull gold or silver. Small boxes like these make superb presents once filled with pot pourri, and when they reach their destination are perfectly good enough to continue in use just as they are.

Another idea for a pot-pourri container might be a simple glass apothecary jar, which can be put to good use once the pot pourri has been removed, or a pretty piece of china filled with a colourful mixture and wrapped up in cellophane. Old cigar boxes can sometimes be bought cheaply and, once thoroughly aired, covered with paper or fabric and filled with a suitably masculine pot pourri.

Last but not least, a very simple way of presenting a scoop of pot pourri might be to put it in a home-made envelope or folder sealed with an adhesive label or a flamboyant blob of sealing wax. A nice finishing touch would be to label the mixture with an evocative name and a suggestion for its use and storage.

LEFT: All kinds of ready-covered boxes are available that make superb containers for home-made pot pourris. Take care, though, to colour-coordinate the contents with the box.

This simple wooden box filled with a colourful pot-pourri mixture has a handful of dried poppy seed-heads glued firmly to the lid for a handle and decoration in one.

A
DIFFERENT TWIST

A very inexpensive but effective way of gift-wrapping pot pourri is to place one or more scoopfuls on a piece of triple-thickness tissue paper, bring the edges up to the middle and tie them with string or ribbon, making a little bag. You can colour-coordinate the pot pourri with the wrapping and add a matching label or gift tag. A pretty touch is to attach a single dried flower, perhaps even a small cluster, to the string or ribbon securing the bag.

A variation on this theme is to use bridal veiling instead of tissue paper. Again, put a scoopful or two of pot pourri in the middle of a double-thickness square of net and bring the edges in to the middle. Tie them with a ribbon and perhaps add a loop, and you will have an instant sweet bag to hang in a cupboard or place in a drawer. A little group of these or the paper twists would look wonderful packed in a small basket with no other wrapping necessary except perhaps a bow on the handle,

and if jazzed up with bright ribbons would be very suitable for a teenage girl, more so probably than a classic, ultra-feminine assortment of flowery fabric sachets and sweet bags.

This method of wrapping something loose can be used for other things, such as the scented flower teas on page 72, or home-made herb mixtures and tisanes. Keep a stock of a few wrapping materials such as tissue paper, ribbon and labels so that you can make quick presents whenever the need arises.

RIGHT: Scoopfuls of pot pourri can simply be wrapped in tissue paper and decorated with dried flowers.

BELOW: Stiff nylon net is the perfect material for instant scented bags that need no further wrapping.

INDEX

Figures printed in **bold** indicate illustrations

CREDITS
With the exception of the photographs listed below, all photographs in this book are by Di Lewis © Salamander Books Ltd.
Guy Rycart © Salamander Books Ltd: 1, 2–3, 4–5, 6–7, 8–9, 22–23, 44–45, 78–79, 116–117, 126–127. Salamander Books Library: 10, 12 (bottom), 15. Colour artwork by Kate Osborne © Salamander Books Ltd. Index by Peter Moloney.